Speak Up!

Speak Up!

DEBATE AND PUBLIC SPEAKING IN HIGH SCHOOL

KATE SHUSTER AND JOHN MEANY

International Debate Education Association
New York, Brussels & Amsterdam

Published by
International Debate Education Association
P.O. Box 922
New York, NY 10009

Copyright © 2015 by International Debate Education Association

This book is published with the generous support of the Open Society Foundations.

Library of Congress Cataloging-in-Publication Data
Shuster, Kate, 1974-
  Speak up! : debate and public speaking in high school / Kate Shuster and John
Meany.
     pages cm
  Includes bibliographical references.
  ISBN 978-1-61770-098-9
  1. Debates and debating. 2. Public speaking. I. Meany, John. II. International Debate
Education Association, issuing body. III. Title.
  PN4181.S534 2014
  808.53071'2--dc23
                              2014031646

Design by Kathleen Hayes
Printed in the USA

 IDEBATE Press

CONTENTS

PREFACE

This text is designed to help teachers and students in secondary schools practice rigorous debating in class and competition. It supports participation in the Public Debate Program, an educational outreach initiative of the Claremont Colleges Debate Union, centered at Claremont McKenna College. The Public Debate Program is the largest, fastest growing and most academically rigorous debate promotion effort in the world, with programming in 20 countries and in many hundreds of schools across the United States.

The Public Debate Program began by targeting students in the middle grades with the Middle School Public Debate Program and expanded to upper secondary students with the High School Public Debate Program. Any student in the Public Debate Program, regardless of grade level, can use this text, although it is primarily targeted at high school students.

In the 15 years that we have been writing together, we have shared a common understanding of debate education: that debate should be easy to learn but challenging to master. We hope that *Speak Up!* puts this shared philosophy into practice. Any teacher, regardless of prior experience, should be able to use this book to teach debating in any subject area. Any student should be able to learn basic and advanced debating skills by using this text.

We have consciously chosen to avoid specialized terminology associated with some debate formats, as jargon can be unnecessarily alienating and intimidating for newcomers. As a result, this text serves as a primer not just for the Public Debate Program format, but for any other debate format as well. Debating changes from region to region, and from nation to nation, but the essential principles of good debating should remain the same.

We wish to acknowledge the many thousands of debaters and teachers who have shaped our understanding of debate education. Their constant push for rigor and accessibility in programming has made the Public Debate Program what it is today.

Information about the program, including competitive opportunities and professional development for educators, is online at www.middle schooldebate.com and www.highschooldebate.org.

SECTION 1:

THE PUBLIC DEBATE PROGRAM

CHAPTER 1:

UNDERSTANDING DEBATE

What is a debate? In everyday speech we often use *debate* to mean many things. It could be an argument—an oral disagreement you might have with a friend—or a discussion of opinions among your fellow students in a history class. These debates are likely to be informal, with few rules and structures. Students don't have training in public speaking or argumentation and the teacher doesn't offer feedback on the students' communication skills.

In contrast, a formal debate is an organized public argument on a specific topic. It is "organized" in that it follows the rules of debating. It is "public" because it is done for the benefit of an audience (even if that audience is only one judge). Debate involves thoroughly explained opinions, which are called "arguments," and addresses a specific topic, with one side arguing in favor of the issue and the other side against it. Formal debating employs critical thinking and communications skills. In these debates, persuasive speaking, topic research, argumentation, and refutation are on display.

Formal competitive debate has four characteristics:

- **Formal debates have rules designed to ensure fairness.** Each side has the same amount of time to present their ideas. Because debating is an educational tool, teams cannot choose which position they argue—they must research both sides of an issue. Nor can they change sides during the debate.

- **Formal debates are based on formal arguments.** Arguments are not just opinions—they are opinions that are explained, justified, and verified. Formal arguments have an assertion (opinion) supported by reason and evidence. For example, you may say that you "had an argument" with your sister:

  You: It is your turn to take out the trash.

  Your sister: No it's not. It's your turn.

  You: No it isn't. It's your turn!

  Your sister: Is not!!

  You: Is too!!!

  The above is not an argument as a debater would define it because your assertions are not supported with reasoning and evidence. You had a simple disagreement over a fact. Neither you nor your sister offered reasoning ("because it is Wednesday, and Wednesday is your day to take out the trash") or evidence ("for example, you took out the trash last Wednesday, when it was your turn") to buttress your assertion. In debate, participants are expected to complete their assertions with reasoning and examples.

- **Formal debate has the expectation of clash.** Ideas "clash" when they directly oppose each other in conflicting and competing ways. Sometimes we exchange ideas that are unrelated:

  You: I like apples because they crunch when you bite into them.

  Your brother: I like oranges because they are fun to peel.

  Both you and your brother have exchanged viewpoints. These are even supported by reasoning (no evidence, though). But they do not clash. Both can be true and you can move forward with your various fruit preferences intact. This is not a debate—only an exchange of ideas. Clash is essential to effective debate to be able to weigh and compare the two sides against each other.

- **In formal debate, an objective party resolves the dispute.** After a formal debate, the judge (or judges) will declare that one side has won the exchange.

Debating Is Like a Trial

To understand how debate works, we can compare it with a criminal trial. A criminal trial has two sides: the prosecution and the defense. The prosecutor's job is to prove that the defendant is guilty of a crime. To do so, she will present a case, selecting those facts, from among all the facts available, that will support her position. She will organize this information and attempt to present it in a compelling manner in an effort to convince the judge or jury that the defendant is guilty.

The defense attorney will argue against the prosecution's case. At trial, the defense will try to show that the prosecution was wrong; he might also bring in new information to try to undermine the prosecution's case—for example, by showing that the defendant could not have been at the scene when the crime was committed. The defense's job is clear: to show that the prosecution has failed to prove its case.

After the trial, a jury will decide the guilt or innocence of the defendant. Although jurors will consider all the facts and arguments presented in the case, their ruling is based on one criterion—whether, given the arguments presented by the defense, the prosecutor has proved her case. If she has proved it beyond a reasonable doubt, then the defendant is guilty and will be sentenced. If she has failed to prove it, then the defendant will go free.

Formal debate is based on this model. Just as in a trial court, formal debate has two sides. The side responsible for supporting the topic is called the "proposition." The other side is called the "opposition." The debate begins with a topic, sometimes called a "motion," for debate. The motion is usually a simple declarative sentence such as "Television is a bad influence" or "The United States should abolish the death penalty." Like the prosecution, the proposition must select from the available arguments to make a case for the motion. They try to show that the motion is more likely to be true than to be false. The opposition will try to undermine this case by challenging it directly as well as by bringing up relevant new information. At the end of the debate, the judge will decide whether, given the arguments made by the proposition, the topic is more likely to be true than false. The wording we've used in comparing a trial and a debate is important. Unlike the prosecutor, the proposition team does not have to prove its case beyond a reasonable doubt. They simply have to show that their arguments are better than the opposition's.

COMPONENTS OF DEBATE

Debate formats have very few rules, but various formats have different conventions that have developed over time. These often are imbedded in the expectations of the judges. Judges may believe that debaters should make a certain number of arguments or advance their ideas in a certain order. When debaters violate these expectations, they risk being marked down for their performances. While this may be unfair, it is an inevitable part of human communication—we are often skeptical or afraid or dismissive of what is foreign or unfamiliar to us. Extraordinary debaters are the ones who *make* the conventions rather than follow them.

Like chess, debating is simple to learn but difficult to master. You might debate through high school and college and even afterward and still find that you have not perfected your skills. So, debate is both fun and challenging. Although arguments and ideas recur from one topic to the next and from one debate to the next, each debate is different and difficult in its own way. Because debate has few rules, a new student can begin debating immediately and find it fun and engaging; experienced debaters can also continue to learn and grow in their practice.

The Process

Every formal debate format has at least four major components: topics for debate, defined sides and an order of speeches, responsibilities for each speaker, and a process for evaluating or judging the debate.

A debate begins with a topic, a focused set of ideas used to direct a discussion to a specific subject. Some topics are far too broad for debating because they involve many different issues. For example, "U.S. History" is a topic—it is a focused set of ideas—but involves many hundreds of important people, places, and events and so is not appropriate for debate. Debates focus on narrow topics so debaters can concentrate on a few key issues.

In the Public Debate Program, each debate involves a different topic. The topic might be "Cigarettes should be illegal," "Viruses are alive," or "The United States is winning the war on terror." Like the prosecutor analyzing and ordering her evidence, the proposition debaters try to identify two to four strong arguments to make a persuasive case. The case is the proof that the topic statement is more likely to be true than false.

The opposition team attempts to prove that the proposition has not made a convincing case. They try to find holes in the proposition team's reasoning and evidence and may also introduce their own arguments to prove that the proposition case is wrong or even dangerous.

A debate judge will listen to the arguments from both teams, consider the reasoning and evidence each team has offered in support of their arguments, and determine which team has won the debate. This decision is based strictly on the arguments presented and challenged; the judge does not let his own knowledge or opinions influence the decision. The judge also assigns an individual score to each debater; this score validates the public speaking and argumentation skills of each individual.

Debating involves comparing and contrasting the arguments of one side with the arguments of the opposing side. Clear and convincing comparisons make debates and their outcomes relatively easy to understand. One side is simply ahead of the other—they have proven their case or overwhelmed their opponent's.

Formats

Students worldwide debate in a variety of formats. These formats differ in the number of participants, the amount of time allowed for research and preparation, the subjects debated, how the debate is conducted (the number, length, and order of speeches), and how the debate is evaluated (debates may be judged by a single person, several individuals as a judging panel or debate jury, or an entire audience). Even the question of which side wins can vary according to the format and its rules for judging and scoring.

The most popular debate formats have something in common—they are all parliamentary debate. That is, they use elements of parliamentary procedure. Public Debate Program debates are sometimes called "parliamentary debate" because they use an element of parliamentary procedure called a "point of information." This chapter will orient you to the rules of the Public Debate Program's format. Remember, though, that a debate format is just that—a format. It does not—and should not—dictate the content and quality of your arguments.

THE PDP FORMAT

PDP debate involves two teams of three speakers who make presentations in the following order:

Speaker	Maximum Speech Time
First speaker, proposition	6 minutes

First speaker, opposition	6 minutes
Second speaker, proposition	6 minutes
Second speaker, opposition	6 minutes
Rebuttal speaker, opposition (also known as the third speaker, opposition)	5 minutes
Rebuttal speaker, proposition (also known as the third speaker, proposition)	5 minutes

Each speaker has a specific role and duties to help organize, explain, and succeed in a debate. But debates are unpredictable and dynamic. A team cannot be sure of their opponent's strategy or what their opponent will argue until speeches are actually delivered. So, debaters must be flexible. They must be prepared to abandon scripted strategies and adapt to the arguments of their opponent. Accordingly, roles and responsibilities could change or might need to be passed to a teammate for her speech. The speaker roles described below are the primary ones for most debates.

First Speaker, Proposition

The opening speaker of the debate establishes the foundation for the entire contest. This speaker interprets the topic, defines key terms, and explains what the topic means for the purposes of the debate. She presents the case—her team's basic stand on the issue—and makes clear what the proposition team must prove to win. She is likely to provide a brief history of the topic, thus ensuring that the judge understands the nature of the problem and has enough background to put subsequent arguments in context. She would then offer between two and four major arguments to establish the case convincingly. These issues will have enough detail so that any single one might be sufficient to win the debate for the proposition team. If the proposition proposes a plan (a solution for an ongoing problem), the speaker includes this, usually after the history.

First Speaker, Opposition

The opposition speaker will use direct and/or indirect arguments to promote clash with the proposition case. The opposition does not have to refute every point the proposition speaker made to put his team in a winning position, but he should account for all her major arguments. The first opposition speaker should say something about each of these issues, even if it is a brief explanation of why he will not formally refute a particular argument.

The opposition has more flexibility to pick and choose arguments than the proposition team, who must defend the core arguments of its case. The first opposition speaker can introduce arguments in the opening speech, testing the proposition and searching for weaknesses. The first opposition speaker presents all major arguments for his side. Because the proposition has the last say, they have an advantage in addressing any argument that develops over the course of the debate. Thus, the opposition must be aggressive and introduce major arguments early so that they are fully understood and convincingly won before the final speech of the debate. Arguments that are still being debated in the final speech are usually decided in the proposition team's favor. By the end of his speech, the first opposition speaker wants to leave the impression for the judge that he has effectively managed the debate for the opposition team.

If possible, this speaker should use the outline structure of the opening proposition speaker. A judge will have recorded that structure in her notes—using the same organizational template helps all participants follow the debate.

Second Speaker, Proposition

The second speaker has two primary duties: defending the case presented by her partner and winning the debate by eliminating opposition arguments from consideration. The speaker may add additional evidence and provide further explanation of the significance of her side's opening arguments to increase their detail and authority. Like the opening opposition speaker, the second proposition speaker should acknowledge all arguments of the opposition, although she may choose to clash with and refute only a select number.

The second proposition speaker delivers a constructive speech and so is entitled to introduce new arguments. Nevertheless, except for an unusual circumstance, she should not do so for three reasons. First, the speaker usually has little time to defend the case and answer objections from the opposition. The presentation of new arguments takes time from these important tasks. Second, keeping the integrity of the case and eliminating challenges from the opposition is more important for winning than is adding arguments. Finally, expanding the debate works in the opposition's favor. Only three speeches remain after this speech—two of which belong to the opposition. Thus, the opposition has enough time to counter new arguments while the proposition's final speaker might not have enough time to rebut the opposition and frame the debate for her side.

Second proposition speakers should function like rebuttalists, carefully selecting issues and reducing the scope of the debate. This approach helps the judge appreciate the detail of their arguments and compare arguments made by the teams.

Second Speaker, Opposition

This speaker has the same responsibilities as the second speaker for the proposition. He must reestablish the winning positions expressed by his teammate in the opening speech and account for and answer any replies from the proposition.

The second opposition speaker might abandon one or more of the arguments the first opposition speaker presented to concentrate on the key issues that will give his team an edge, but he must make sure the judge does not think that his failure to address an argument is an oversight. If he wants to abandon an argument, he should note this to the judge. The judge needs to realize that the speaker is conceding the argument intentionally as a tactical move. It is an act of commission, not an act of omission.

The Opposition Block

The opposition team has back-to-back speeches in the debate. The second opposition constructive speech is immediately followed by the third opposition speech, the opposition rebuttal speech. These speeches, often referred to as "the opposition block," dominate the center of the debate. This block of time and the opposition team's ability to control the center of the debate balances the proposition team's advantage in presenting the first and last speeches.

The second opposition constructive and rebuttal speeches function like one long speech, a final stand for the opposition team. It is appropriate, for example, for the second opposition speaker to identify four major arguments in the debate and say, "In my speech, I will address the first three issues; my partner will manage the final one and summarize our team's position in his rebuttal." The opposition rebuttalist is not permitted to introduce new arguments; however, because the arguments from the second proposition speaker have a foundation in the constructive speeches in the debate, the opposition rebuttalist is not introducing a new argument when replying to the issues.

If the opposition does not effectively use the opposition block, the team will be ceding preparation time to their opponents.

Rebuttal Speaker, Opposition

The rebuttal speeches are summary speeches in the debate. Speakers use this final speech to make their best argument about why their team has won the debate.

If using the block, the opposition speaker should address the final major issue for his team. The speaker should then select from among the major arguments in the debate and work to convince the judge that one or two tip the debate to the opposition side. (This speaker might be able to manage a third major issue as well.) This speaker must remember that the debate is ending. At this point, issues need to be resolved in the opposition's favor. Thus, using this speech to continue focusing on the details of the issues raised in the debate will usually help the proposition team because they have the final say.

Rebuttal Speaker, Proposition

This speaker has the same role as the opposition rebuttal speaker and should follow the guidelines for that speaker. She should extend the proposition's most effective argument, refute the opposition team's arguments, and summarize the debate for her side. She must explain to the judge how the proposition side has made and sustained their case and, therefore, won the debate.

Debate Tournaments

Students have the opportunity to participate in debates not only in the classroom or public settings but also in debate tournaments. A tournament is a focused competition featuring students from many schools competing in a series of debates. Tournaments may last one or more days, but the typical high school PDP event is usually held on a single Saturday or Sunday. Tournaments are fun and challenging and offer opportunities to debate students from many backgrounds.

Debaters attend as three-person teams from the same school. You may choose your teammates or your coach may assign you partners, depending on your school's policy. You participate as a team throughout the competition. You will never debate students from your own school nor will you debate before a judge from your school. For most tournament competitions, schools can enter more than one team. The limit on entries is set by the number of participating schools and the classroom space available at the tournament site. At some PDP tournaments, for example, schools may bring 4 or 5 teams; at other events, they can register 14 or 15.

Tournament debates are judged by adults from all walks of life. You may debate before teachers, attorneys, business owners, bus drivers, parents, state and federal judges, college students, or retired community volunteers.

A day of debating usually begins with morning registration followed by a series of four or five debates and then awards. Awards are normally given in several categories: team performance, individual performance, top individual performance from each attending school, and school performance. Special award categories may have been established for newly participating schools or smaller schools. Team awards are given to the team who won the most debates. In case of a tie, the team with the highest total of individual points wins. Individual awards are based on students' total scores for the day. School awards may recognize schools with the most total wins or the highest average wins for the day.

Some schools combine to form leagues. Leagues allow schools to pool their resources to offer a series of monthly competitions (usually five or six) during the academic year. Information about forming a league is available on the Public Debate Program's website: http://highschool debate.org/.

CHAPTER 2:
RULES FOR PDP COMPETITIVE DEBATING

The Public Debate Program is designed to be a comprehensive educational debating program for students in middle school and high school. With a few exceptions having to do with speaking time and topic selection, the rules for middle school debating apply to high school, so the transition from middle to secondary school debates is basically seamless. In addition, training for coaches, judges, and debaters is similar. The assessment rubric for high school and middle school students focuses on developing the same public speaking, argumentation, and refutation skills.

The Public Debate Program *Rules for Competition* covers the eight key areas of a debate.

- Debate topics

- Number of teams and debaters

- Speaking order and speaking time limits

- Preparation period

- Debate materials

- Points of information and heckling

- Judge training and decision making

- After the debate

Much of the material covered in the rules is also discussed elsewhere in this book, but it is important that you understand the rationale behind the rules if you are to get the most benefit from participating in the PDP program.

Debate Topics

THE RULES

High school PDP competitions use a mix of prepared (extemporaneous) and impromptu motions. Each debate has a different topic. A prepared topic is announced several weeks (generally four) in advance of a competition. This gives debaters time to think about the topic; research and analyze arguments for and against it; and carefully organize notes on the strongest arguments. An impromptu topic is not announced until 30 minutes before the debate is to begin. Once the topic is announced, debaters draw on their own knowledge, with help from their coaches, to plan arguments and anticipate the other side's ideas.

UNDERSTANDING THE RULES

During a semester or competition season, you will debate a variety of social and political issues. You are expected to research and learn about both sides of each topic because sides are assigned shortly before a debate begins. Consequently, over the course of a season, you will become familiar with the major arguments and issues on each side of many current controversies, building a knowledge base that will help you become an informed citizen.

The topics you will debate follow PDP guidelines for selection and phrasing. Although you will not have to formulate a topic, understanding the reasoning behind how topics are developed will help you debate. Those individuals developing topics are guided by the following rules:

- **Topics should be simple, declarative sentences** such as "Extra-terrestrial intelligence exists" or "Schools should not serve junk food." Clarity helps you understand which issues support the topic and those arguments that might effectively clash with the proposition team's case.

- **Topics should encourage the application of higher-level thinking skills.** They may use comparative language, (e.g., "On balance, video games do more good than harm") or complex terms (e.g., "It is unethical to eat meat") to help you develop critical thinking skills.

- **Topics should be challenging, serious issues of local, regional, national, or international concern.** While debating about whether Batman could defeat Superman (hint: Batman will probably lose) or whether a dog makes a better pet than cat may be fun, PDP debates focus on topics such as federal bailouts of banks, the application of economic sanctions as a tool of foreign policy, abolition of supermajority voting in legislatures, and military intervention to help you better understand what is going on in your world.

- **Topics should be age-appropriate.** PDP topics involve issues of interest to your age group.

- **Where possible, topics should intersect with the school curriculum.** Topics are often drawn from what you are studying in the classroom.

- **Topics should be chosen and approved by teachers.** Your teachers have the best idea of what you can do and what you are learning.

- **Topics should be fair to both teams.** They should not ask too much of one team while making it much easier for the other team to win. They avoid extreme language like "always," "never" and "all," which makes the topic nearly impossible for the proposition to prove in a relatively brief debate.

- **Topics should avoid false dichotomies.** A false dichotomy occurs when a topic poses a choice when, in fact, a choice need not be made. A topic such as "Citizens should give up freedom for safety" makes it proportionately much easier for the opposition to win as they must only prove that citizens need not make such a choice.

Number of Teams and Debaters

THE RULES

Each PDP debate has two teams: proposition and opposition. Each debate team has three students: the first and second speakers for the team and a third speaker, also known as the rebuttal speaker. Each team debates together throughout a competition without substitutions. If, for some reason, only two students are able to make up a team (for example, if the third team member becomes ill), those two may participate as a team. In that case, the team member who speaks first also delivers the third speech, the rebuttal speech. The missing student on the team receives an individual score of zero.

UNDERSTANDING THE RULES

The Public Debate Program uses teams of three because of the educational and social benefits of working in larger groups. Teams of three also teach you to work in more complex team environments, thus helping you learn the valuable negotiation and compromise skills that are important to work in school and in professional contexts. Working in a three-person team forces you to persuade at least one other member of the team to agree with you to settle any team-based decision—speaker position for each of the teammates, strategy and tactics for debates, etc. The three-person team creates an opportunity for you and your colleagues to practice debating (argumentation and persuasion) during debate preparation as well as in formal debates. Finally, working in teams of three helps beginning debaters, who can learn from their more experienced teammates.

Speaking Order and Speaking Time Limits

THE RULES

Speakers make their presentations in the following order. The time listed is the maximum for each speech.

First Speaker, Proposition Team	6 minutes
First Speaker, Opposition Team	6 minutes
Second Speaker, Proposition Team	6 minutes
Second Speaker, Opposition Team	6 minutes
Rebuttal Speaker, Opposition Team	5 minutes
Rebuttal Speaker, Proposition Team	5 minutes

The first four speeches are sometimes called "constructive speeches." In these speeches, each team will construct, or build, its arguments. New arguments may be introduced in any of these speeches. The final two speeches of the debate are called "rebuttal speeches." These are summary speeches. In these speeches, the debaters try to offer the best comparative conclusion for their side of the debate and, at the same time, try to eliminate the major points of the other team.

Judges are told to disregard new arguments offered in rebuttal speeches. New arguments are defined as arguments without a foundation in the constructive speeches. For example, if the debate were about health care policy and a concluding speaker offered new ideas about how U.S. health care policy would affect foreign aid to Africa, the judge would consider it a new argument because it had no relation to the arguments in the constructive speeches. She would ignore it in her evaluation of the debate.

UNDERSTANDING THE RULES

The proposition team opens and closes the debate because they have the burden of proof in a debate: they must prove the motion is **more** true than false. The proposition team's job is harder than the opposition's because it is always more difficult to build something than to tear it down. For balance, the PDP format gives the opposition two speeches in a row—the second opposition speech and the opposition rebuttal are back-to-back. As we have seen, these two speeches function as a unit, with each adding its own material, summation, and ideas to the debate. Consequently, the last speech—by the proposition rebuttalist— is the most difficult in the debate because the speaker must respond to 11 minutes of opposition team material in addition to reinforcing her team's ideas—all in just 5 minutes.

The debate becomes more complicated as it proceeds. It begins with a case for the motion. The next speaker refutes the case and brings in new ideas. Each subsequent speaker continues the process of refutation while keeping the team's ideas afloat. The final speakers are responsible for making sense of the debate in a way that will encourage the judge to vote for their side—this requires cleverness and careful note taking.

The Preparation Period

THE RULES

Teams are assigned a side (proposition or opposition), an opponent, and a judge before each debate. Tournament officials then distribute colored paper for use during the preparation period. A different color is used for each debate. After the teams have received their paper, the topic is announced. If the topic has been announced before the tournament or competition (an extemporaneous topic), debaters have 20 minutes of preparation time to review their notes, speak with their coaches and teammates, and copy notes or other information onto the colored paper. If the topic is impromptu, debaters have 30 minutes to prepare. Debaters may use this time to prepare notes and outlines for use in the debate, but they are prohibited from reading prepared speeches during the debate.

UNDERSTANDING THE RULES

The preparation period is to be used to develop your team's ideas in advance of the debate. Of course, you will have done much of this work before you reach the tournament.

The rules prohibit reading prepared speeches for several reasons. First, the prohibition forces you to digest the research you have done before the competition. If you know that you will not be able to read prepared speeches, you will focus on thoroughly understanding the material. Second, prohibiting prepared speeches helps to "level the playing field." Debaters cannot read speeches that others have written for them, so they must express their own ideas. Finally, the prohibition also encourages you to develop the skills needed for professional communication. Very few people will ever be asked to deliver a speech that they can read from a manuscript. Also, for most over the age of 10, being read to is quite boring. Effective speakers are able to talk from a limited set of notes and express their own ideas—the preparation period helps debaters to practice this skill.

Colored paper simply helps to ensure fair play. If all notes used in the debate are written on the same color paper, there is no question about whether notes were written prior to the start of the preparation time.

Debate Materials

THE RULES

Before a debate tournament or competition or during preparation time, students may review any information they think would help them prepare for a debate. This includes books, newspaper or magazine articles on current events, class notes, and written records of debate meetings and previous debates. They may speak to teachers, coaches, teammates, parents, friends—anyone they choose. Debaters may not use computers or other mechanical devices unless they have been granted permission in advance of the competition for reasons of equity related to a disability. Coaches and parents assisting debaters during preparation time also may not consult electronic resources.

Once the debate begins, debaters may not review or use any notes that were not prepared during the preparation period. Using pre-prepared materials in the debate is a serious violation of the rules and may result in a student forfeiting or losing the debate.

UNDERSTANDING THE RULES

During preparation, you may consult any materials you have brought to the debate, although you may not use your computer. You may also receive coaching from teachers, volunteer coaches, and parents; this is best done, however, before attending the tournament. For the best results, you should work almost exclusively with your teammates during preparation time.

You should write your own notes. This ensures not only that you can read them but also that a well-meaning adult has not written them. Your parents or coach want to help you win, but you don't learn debating and communication skills if they do the work.

Using or reviewing too many materials in the preparation period can be a disadvantage. The most successful debaters have already read and digested their research prior to the tournament and made outlines or other easily copied materials. Over time, you will learn what techniques work best for you.

Points of Information and Heckling

THE RULES

A point of information (also known as a POI, pronounced "P-O-I") is an interjection by a speaker's opponents to make a comment or ask a question. POIs are directed only to a member of the opposing team; a debater may not request a POI during a teammate's speech.

Debaters can offer POIs only during the middle minutes of the constructive speeches (the first two speeches of both teams). The first and last minute of these speeches is "protected time," when the speaker is shielded from inquiries from the other side. The judge will signal the beginning and end of protected time by slapping the table once. Debaters cannot offer POIs in the rebuttal speeches (the last two speeches).

A debater applies for a POI by standing and saying "Information" or "Point of Information." The speaker may accept it or reject it. If she rejects it, she indicates this by gently waving a hand downward, signaling that the opponent should sit, or by saying "No, thank you." The speaker can use either method, although the the hand gesture is preferred as it is less disruptive for the speaker. If she accepts the POI, the speaker simply says "Yes" or "I'll take your point."

More than one person on a team can request a point of information at any one time. A rejection by the speaker applies to all opponents attempting a point at that time.

If the speaker accepts a point, the opposing team's point may not last longer than 15 seconds. The speaker accepts only a single point at a time. The person making a POI may not interrupt the speaker's answer, ask a two-part question, ask a follow-up question, or make any other comment unless the speaker agrees to it by accepting another point of information.

A heckle is an interruption of a speaker during her presentation. Heckles are designed to communicate brief but meaningful information about an issue to the judge. The PDP format encourages responsible heckling. Debaters heckle to applaud teammates and opponents before and after their speeches as a sign of respect and support for participating in a difficult competition. Debaters may also cheer the good arguments of their teammates by pounding the table and shouting "Hear! Hear!" They may show their displeasure with an opponent's speech by saying "Shame!"

Heckles may be only one or two words. Disruptive heckling, defined as four or more words or interruptions that are nonargumentative, is not permitted.

UNDERSTANDING THE RULES

The PDP format has no rules about how many POIs you should accept (a guideline is to accept at least two). Similarly, no rules are in place about how many points you should offer (but participants should attempt to make points as appropriate). If you take so many points that your speech becomes unfocused and confusing, you have lost control of the floor and will be scored accordingly. Similarly, if you do not take and respond to at least a couple POIs, you have failed to demonstrate mastery of the format and will be scored accordingly.

Points of information and heckling are included in the PDP format to encourage impromptu argumentation and the development of advanced public speaking skills. They make the debate exciting, interactive, and fun. You can use these techniques to remain involved in the debate both before and after your speech. Because heckling is permitted in all speeches, it also provides the opposition team an opportunity to offer a brief but necessary rejoinder during the proposition rebuttal (the last speech in the debate). Using POIs and heckling ensure that both teams are included in all speeches in the debate.

POIs and heckling must be used carefully to communicate with the judge and may never be used to distract a speaker or continually interrupt a presentation. The judge may reward individual speakers and teams for the effective use of points of information and heckling. Rude behavior will result in a low score.

Judge Training and Decision Making

THE RULES

Every Public Debate Program judge must be certified to judge at competitions. College students and other adults are eligible to become judges, but high school students cannot judge high school debates.

Judges are expected to decide the outcome of a debate carefully and impartially. If a judge believes she cannot decide a debate fairly, she must remove herself from judging. Judges are never assigned to hear debates by students from their own school. Judges must take notes using a flowsheet (explained in Chapter 7) and are responsible for ensuring accurate timing of the debate.

The judge must decide the winning side of the debate—the team that argued successfully on the topic. There are no ties. If the proposition team proves its case for the motion, the judge should reward them, if not, the win goes to the opposition.

In addition to deciding the winning team, a judge must award individual points to each debater. Participants are rated on a scale of 0–100 points, with 100 awarded for a perfect performance. The judge considers public speaking, argumentation, and teamwork skills in assigning individual speaker points. Judges must use the official high school PDP rubric (see Appendix 3) to assign points. A judge may give the same number of points to more than one participant.

After careful deliberation, the judge will complete a ballot, a record of the debate given to her by the tournament host. On the ballot, she provides a detailed description of the reasons for her decision and gives additional comments to help debaters improve. She will then announce the outcome of the debate to the participating teams. She also will explain the reasons why a particular side won and provide some constructive oral criticism.

UNDERSTANDING THE RULES

The Public Debate Program is the only debating program in the United States that requires training and certification of judges. It is also unique in requiring the judge to reveal and explain the decision to participants at the conclusion of every debate. At first, insisting on disclosure might seem odd—after all, in a soccer game, officials don't hide who made goals. But in nearly all secondary school debate formats in the United States, judges do not have to reveal debate results to students or give feedback to assist students in future performances. Consequently, many do not.

The PDP strongly believes in the educational and social values of transparency. You learn best when judges fully reveal their rationales and offer feedback to help you hone your public speaking and argumentation skills for future debates. Also, you are more likely to fully absorb their comments immediately after the debate when your speech is still firmly in your mind.

Transparency encourages judges to be accountable for their decisions. A judge is more likely to consider the arguments from both sides when she must explain her decision to both teams. Finally, announcing the outcome of each debate helps correct errors in tournament results. Although errors are infrequent, they do happen. Disclosure of the debate results can help students and schools get the right awards for their performances.

After the Debate

THE RULES

Once the debate is over, participants are encouraged to discuss the results with the judge and ask her advice on how to improve their debating skills. No debater is permitted to dispute the judge's decision, however. If a participant has a complaint about a judge's behavior during the debate, he should speak to his coach, who may then raise the matter with the appropriate tournament officials.

UNDERSTANDING THE RULES

A judge's decision is final. To proceed otherwise is to undermine the system of mutual and professional respect that makes debating programs possible. Judges are human. Thus, each one may watch a debate and make a slightly different decision for slightly different reasons. At first, this may seem unfair. But judging debates is more art than science. All educated people do not listen to a politician's speech and arrive at the same opinion. Why? Because communication is a complicated enterprise. Successful debaters are able to win no matter who is judging; blaming a poor performance on judging is a beginner's mistake.

DEBATE ESSENTIALS

CHAPTER 3:
PUBLIC SPEAKING

Effective public speaking is essential for debaters, who must persuade a decision maker: a judge. The skills developed and practiced in debate will benefit you in other areas of your life. Practicing and refining these skills will help you succeed in college and internship interviews, class and roundtable discussions, extemporaneous and PowerPoint presentations, in leadership roles in clubs and organizations, and in your career. Public speaking helps you develop self-confidence, independence, and resilience; improves your ability to engage others in the processes of critical thinking, agenda setting, and decision making; and prepares you for academic and career leadership and success.

Persuasive public speakers blend the appropriate arguments with a clear and confident style of delivery. They show mastery of the subject matter in their presentation of information. They are informative and entertaining. They employ many different public speaking techniques, including organized and logical arguments, careful, proper use of words, simple and direct messages, powerful images, and interesting vocal delivery. Effective speakers research and know their topics, anticipate opponents' arguments, and readily, almost seamlessly, adapt to them.

There is no best way to deliver a speech. Trying to copy the style of more experienced or successful debaters is a mistake. Talented, experienced speakers each have different styles. Although they are all known as highly effective public speakers, Dr. Martin Luther King, Jr., Winston Churchill, Gov. Ann Richards, Pres. Barack Obama, Justice Sonia

Sotomayor, and Stephen Colbert do not and did not deliver speeches in the same way. Develop your own effective style. You want to make a better version of a presentation than your opponents, not merely mirror the performances of others.

You learn public speaking just as you would any other new skill—by identifying your natural strengths and weaknesses and then working to make more effective presentations through regular, patient practice. When you begin your training, make a brief, 2–3 minute presentation and videotape it for later review and analysis. Repeat the process about every four weeks as you gain confidence and skill. Very shortly, you will make and see a remarkable transformation—from an anxious and disorganized to a highly accomplished speaker.

Communication

We communicate to share our opinions and convey our ideas. We do this not only with our voice (verbal communication) but also through the use of our body (nonverbal communication). To be effective communicators, debaters need to be expert at both, utilizing vocal delivery, gestures, and stance to present compelling arguments that keep listeners engaged.

VERBAL COMMUNICATION

Your vocal delivery—how you present your speech—will influence how your audience hears your message. You cannot persuade other people of your opinion if you cannot be heard or if you don't speak confidently. An effective speaker wants her message to be heard and her audience to accept her perspective. In addition, she needs to ensure that the judge understands the substantive details of arguments—that they make sense.

Effectively using volume, pace, and emphasis allows you to highlight the key elements of an argument and establish a convincing narrative that the judge can follow. Utilizing the following verbal communication techniques will make it easier for a judge or audience to pay attention to your speech and appreciate your research, knowledge, and argumentation, thus enhancing your credibility.

Key Verbal Communication Skills

Volume

Pace

Emphasis

Volume

To be effective, speak at a slightly louder volume than you would use in normal conversation. Increased volume expresses your confidence in your ideas; you appear ready to shout out your ideas to get others to follow your lead. You trust yourself to be a vocal advocate of an issue, demonstrating that listeners should trust you as well.

Adapt your volume to the room and your message. Speak more loudly in a larger room and at a more subdued level if the judge or audience is seated only a few feet away. You might lower your volume to express grief, guilt, or concern—or raise it to express anger or excitement. Also, alter your volume during your speech for variety; listeners get bored when hearing a speech delivered at the same volume.

Pace

Pace refers to your rate of delivery. Effective speakers alter their pace, quickening and slowing it to ensure that listeners can understand and record key information.

Your rate of delivery should be slightly faster than your normal conversational rate. It should sound natural and should be fast enough that the judge and audience will remain engaged and will not try to fill in words or start daydreaming. A speech that is just slightly faster than a conversational rate will not be so fast that the judge and audience will not be able to understand the main points of your message nor will they lose track of key opinions or facts.

Vary your pace to create listener interest and highlight key sections or arguments of your presentation. If you are presenting new, technical, or challenging material, speak slowly so that the listeners are able to readily follow your line of reasoning. You also might deliver a section slowly to emphasize a key point. Speakers naturally pause at the conclusion of a sentence or in speech transitions (moving from one major part of a speech to another or from one major argument to another). Consider emphasizing these pauses to slow or "break the pace" of a speech.

Simple repetition and redundancy (use of synonyms and similar expressions to reinforce an idea) are forms of a speech pause. Instead of an actual break in the speech, repetition and redundancy allow you to continue talking while creating a pause. The judge does not have to listen to understand new material. She has time to reflect on and record your argument. Here is an example of varied pace in a speech in which a debater argues that proliferation of nuclear weapons is unlikely to cause a nuclear conflict.

> Since the U.S. development and use of the atomic bomb in 1945, nine countries have produced and tested nuclear weapons. Many of these countries have ongoing hostilities or serious tension with other nuclear powers. But not one country has used a nuclear weapon in a conflict. (*More slowly and clearly, enunciating each word.*) Regardless of international tension or national security concerns, no nuclear power has used a nuclear weapon. (*Now louder, and with more emphasis.*) Not one example in more than almost 70 years!

Some pauses can hurt a speaker's credibility. These are known as "vocalized pauses"—fillers such as "you know" or "umm" that speakers use when they don't know what to say next. Avoid these. Simply pausing is much better than using a filler. Slowing your delivery will often eliminate a substantial number of vocalized pauses.

Emphasis

In debates, speakers emphasize particular words to remind the judge of important key ideas or facts. Following all the details of a debate speech with equal attention is challenging for the audience, so effective speakers highlight the segments that *must* be remembered. They use dramatic language, powerful imagery, and altered tone of voice to make some parts of their speech stand out from others.

You undermine emphasis when you mispronounce words or your pronunciation lacks clarity. If you mispronounce a name or word, the judge might think you are unfamiliar with the person, location, or issue. So, before a debate, practice pronouncing difficult and uncommon words related to your topic.

Common Pronunciation Errors

Correct pronunciation and spelling	*Popular and incorrect pronunciation*
Arctic (ark-tik)	Artic (ar-tik)
formerly (for-mer-lee)	formally (for-mal-lee)
library (lie-brer-ee)	libary (lie-bar-ee)
nuclear (noo-klee-ar)	nucular (noo-kew-lar)
suppose (su-poz)	Susppose(sus-poz)
picture (pik-chur)	piture (pit-chur)
tyranny (tear-an-ee))	tyranny (tie-ran-ee)

NONVERBAL COMMUNICATION

Nonverbal communication, "body language," involves nods, smiles, shrugs, frowns, gestures, and body movement. These subtle communication elements can send powerful signals from one person to another. For example, a speaker can hold the attention of the audience with eye contact and facial expressions that reveal emotions. She can create a powerful presence though use of body position and movement. To effectively persuade, you must consider nonverbal communication as seriously as the verbal content of your message. If you don't, you may risk confusing or alienating your audience.

Body Positioning and Movement

To persuade, you need to see the audience and be seen by them. Effective speakers establish a line-of-sight with the audience. They use their body position, stance, and movement to attract and hold the attention of their listeners.

In a PDP debate, a speaker must be visible to the opposing team (especially for POIs) and the judge. Usually this means standing in the front and center of a room; in some classrooms, though, this may not be the best location. Select the position that makes it easiest for the audience to see you.

Begin your speech in the position you have chosen but, if possible, move to the side of a lectern or desk to deliver your opening section. Lean forward a bit or take a slight step forward to connect with your audience. Remain there, continuing your speech for 45 seconds to 1 minute, before returning to your original position. Your movement will provide the audience a welcome break from watching you stand in one spot. Avoid constant movement or pacing back and forth, however—it can be distracting.

Relax at the beginning of your presentation so you can avoid shifting your weight, which produces a rocking motion. You may be unable to detect these side-to-side movements, but audiences will see them and, unfortunately, they are often all that they will remember. Plant your feet about shoulder width apart and settle into a comfortable stance; then begin your speech. If you are balanced and comfortable, your body movements are more likely to be controlled, poised, and graceful.

Eye Contact

Eye contact is essential to a successful presentation. It is the single most effective nonverbal communication tool you have. It reaches out to an audience and pulls them in, bridging the physical distance between you and your listeners. Eye contact can personalize a speech. You do not have to look at every person in a crowded room during your presentation, but you should look in each direction of the room. Doing so lets listeners know that your message is for everyone, not just those directly in front of you.

When you begin your introduction, look directly at the audience. One of the major errors new speakers make is to look down at notes or away from the audience as they begin their speech. This is like looking at the ground when shaking hands with someone for the first time. It shows a shyness or awkwardness. The audience needs to be welcomed to the speech; looking down disinvites them.

Gestures

Using gestures adds movement to your presentation and helps you emphasize the important points. To become an effective speaker, you have to use them appropriately. Many novice speakers don't know what to do with their hands. Should they clasp them together behind their back, hold on to the side of the lectern or podium, fold their hands in front of their body, use one hand to hold a flowsheet or other notes? All of these might be acceptable for a portion of the speech, but you shouldn't maintain any single position for too long.

Gestures are like the organized movements of actors on a stage. The movement is planned and used to support key features of your speech.

For example, you might point at the audience to stress their responsibility to think some way or do something; flick your hand outward with palm down to dismiss an opponent's POI, or use fingers to tick off the three major points of your speech.

If you are delivering your speech from behind a lectern or podium, keep your gestures above or to the side of the furniture—any movement made behind the lectern is invisible to the audience. If nothing is between you and your audience, gesture within the frame of your body. Movement that is far from your body will make you appear to be out of control.

Organize gestures to match your message. If you refer to a global problem, a broad gesture would add to your point that the issue is universal or all-encompassing. If one issue matters more than all the others in the debate, holding up a single finger for the entire time you discuss that issue would emphasize that "this one is important." Thoughtful gesturing that adds value to the substantive matter, that reinforces the speaker's point, can be compelling.

Avoid aggressive gestures (jabbing a finger at an opponent, furiously shaking one's head in disagreement at an opponent during a POI); they are disrespectful, if not hostile, acts. Don't hold objects such as a pen during your speech. The judge's eye will follow the object, like an orchestra following the conductor's baton, and she will be distracted from what you are saying. But using nods, smiles, and shrugs can work well. For example, a simple nod during a POI lets the judge know that you understand the POI and are setting up an anticipated and more effective clash in a reply.

Teammates may also gesture during a partner's speech. Nods and smiles work well, but don't use them too frequently. The speaker loses credibility and a judge or audience is less likely to think that a particular gesture is meaningful if it is endlessly repeated. Never use very negative gestures (shaking the head indicating "No!!!") during an opponent's speech. It is discourteous and often backfires by producing sympathy for the speaker.

1. Word and Phrase Emphasis

Read each sentence below to emphasize the emotion in parenthesis.

I already told you. *(Frustration)*

I like you. *(Friendly)*

Come back here. *(Anger)*

You did that. *(Surprise)*

I thought he would win. *(Irony)*

2. Letter Groups

Slowly repeat each of the following letter groups:

www, www, www, www, wdw, wdw, www, www, www, wtw, wtw, wtw, www

lll, lll, lwl, lwl, lll, lll, ltl, ltl, lkl, lkl, lll, lll, lwl, lwl, lhl, lhl, ltl, ltl, lkl, lkl, lwl, lwl

www, bbb, ddd, www, kgh, ddd, www, kgh, lwl, www, wdw, lwl, wbw, www

3. Tongue Twisters

Speaking at a conversational or slightly faster rate, repeat each of the following tongue twisters three or four times.

- Greek grapes
- Clean cream can
- Sell thick socks
- Red lorry, yellow lorry
- Thieves seize skis

- Truly rural

- Six thick thistle sticks

- Shredded Swiss cheese

- Knapsack straps

- Which wristwatches are Swiss wristwatches?

- Real weird rear wheels

- One smart fellow, he felt smart. Two smart fellows, they felt smart. Three smart fellows, they all felt smart.

- Pick a partner and practice passing, for if you pass proficiently, perhaps you'll play professionally.

- Mr. See owned a saw. And Mr. Soar owned a seesaw. Now See's saw sawed Soar's seesaw. Before Soar saw See. Which made Soar sore. Had Soar seen See's saw before See sawed Soar's seesaw, See's saw would not have sawed Soar's seesaw. So See's saw sawed Soar's seesaw. But it was sad to see Soar so sore just because See's saw sawed Soar's seesaw!

4. Practice with Unfamiliar Language

One way to improve public speaking is to practice unfamiliar words and phrases. Speaking unfamiliar and unusual words causes you to carefully concentrate on each word and sentence. Read Lewis Carroll's poem, "The Jabberwocky," silently and then practice it aloud.

'Twas brillig, and the slithy toves
Did gyre and gimble in the wabe:
All mimsy were the borogoves,
And the mome raths outgrabe.

"Beware the Jabberwock, my son!
The jaws that bite, the claws that catch!
Beware the Jubjub bird, and shun

The frumious Bandersnatch!"

He took his vorpal sword in hand;
Long time the manxome foe he sought—
So rested he by the Tumtum tree
And stood awhile in thought.

And, as in uffish thought he stood,
The Jabberwock, with eyes of flame,
Came whiffling through the tulgey wood,
And burbled as it came!

One, two! One, two!
And through and through
The vorpal blade went snicker-snack!
He left it dead, and with its head
He went galumphing back.

"And, hast thou slain the Jabberwock?
Come to my arms, my beamish boy!
O frabjous day! Callooh! Callay!"
He chortled in his joy.

'Twas brillig, and the slithy toves
Did gyre and gimble in the wabe:
All mimsy were the borogoves,
And the mome raths outgrabe.

5. Word Choice

Some words and phrases are more likely to persuade because they create vivid and powerful images. They emphasize action, leadership, and forward-thinking. They are routinely used in political and commercial advertising. Deliver a 2–3 minute argument using several of the following words and phrases:

duty	focus	freedom
efficient	forward	guarantee

identity	plan	truth
immediate	prevent	ultimate
implement	progress	urgent
improve	protection	as the evidence shows
innovate	responsibility	at last
justice	security	call to action
key	simplify	important development
liberty	solve	last chance
lifesaving	suddenly	new technique
manage	superior	now is the time
mobilize	tradition	on the brink
overcome	triumph	

Organization—The Narrative Arc of a Speech

To debate successfully, you must do far more than pronounce words properly; you must express your ideas effectively. Your speech should be simple, direct, and clear. It should follow a simple structure and have a logical sequence of ideas.

Well-organized speakers often use a simple narrative structure that has the order in which a story is told. This structure has three parts: an introduction, a main body, and a conclusion.

INTRODUCTION

Your introduction must attract the attention of your listeners and draw them into the speech. You can do this with a dramatic anecdote, a surprising fact, or humor. The introduction should also establish the significance of the speech: *Why should anyone listen?* It should have both a qualitative and quantitative dimension, explaining why your subject matters to your audience (qualitative dimension) and how the issues you will discuss affect a number of people (quantitative dimension). In addition, it should preview or highlight the major elements of your speech. You may introduce yourself near the beginning of a speech, but you should present your attention getter and explain the importance of the issue before you do so.

BODY

The body of your speech should contain two or three major arguments designed to convince the judge that your team is correct about the issue at hand. Don't try to present all potential arguments; you won't have time to address each adequately. Instead, limit your presentation to the more significant ones and present these in a logical order.

You can organize your ideas chronologically; by cause and effect (How did that action lead to that result?); or by problem and solution (What is the ongoing problem? What can we do solve it ?). The logical sequencing of ideas makes a speech easy to follow. Each major point should be well-reasoned and supported with appropriate evidence. The evidence might be in the form of expert testimony, statistical information, contemporary and historical examples, personal experience, or other facts that support reasoning.

With the exception of the opening speaker, each speaker must also consider and reply to issues raised by the opposing team.

CONCLUSION

To be effective, your speech must have a compelling and powerful conclusion. It should remind the audience of your main points and include a short sentence that summarizes the purpose of your presentation. Your conclusion, made in 10–15 seconds, should echo in the room (or inside the judge's mind) after you have taken your seat.

CHAPTER 4:
ARGUMENTATION

Debates are organized formats for public argument. They involve reasoned discourse and provide a structure to identify, explain, justify, verify, and compare opinions. When an opinion is supported by detailed explanation, justification, and verification, it becomes an "argument." To be an effective debater or public speaker, you must be able to make an effective argument.

An argument in a formal debate is not just an expression of simple disagreement nor is it just a powerful articulation of an idea. It is the best possible expression of a defensible idea. Arguments *prove* the position of each side of the debate. The proposition arguments try to clearly establish that the topic is more likely to be true than false; the opposition will try to demonstrate that the proposition case is illegitimate.

The formal arguments used in debate have three parts: assertion, reasoning, and evidence (A-R-E). An assertion is a contention that something is true. Reasoning explains and justifies an assertion; evidence verifies it. Reasons and evidence prove your statements, thus encouraging your audience to agree with your assertion.

Assertion

An assertion is an unsupported statement, an opinion. It is also called a "claim." An assertion is as likely to be right as it is to be wrong; it is no better or worse than any other person's opinion. Typically, our day is filled with assertions, which we are not usually called on to explain or defend. "My favorite color is blue." "I like Daft Punk." "My sandwich was too dry." "It's cold in this room; I need a sweater." All these statements are assertions. Assertions do not give one team an advantage over the other. Any assertion in reply is as valid as the original assertion. The other side will simply offer a counter-assertion, an equivalent, different, and opposing unsupported opinion. In a debate, an assertion might produce a draw but it cannot give you the win.

Reasoning

The second part of a formal argument is reasoning—the logic that supports the assertion. Reasoning is based on your analysis of an opinion. It answers the questions: Why do you hold this opinion? What is your explanation for the opinion? What justification do you have for the opinion? With reasoning, an opinion makes sense.

The reasoning for an opinion is the "because" statement in an argument. A simple assertion is explained with the word *because*. For example, "Schools should require uniforms because doing so reduces the cost of clothing for students." Or "The United States should utilize military action in response to chemical weapons use because doing so will deter governments from using these weapons in the future." Successful debaters have strong explanations for their opinions. They also may have multiple justifications for supporting an assertion. Substantive and multiple reasons increase the likelihood that this part of an argument is defensible.

Evidence

Reasoning is not enough to complete an argument. Debaters must verify that the reasoning they have used is consistent with experience. This requires evidence. Evidence is the proof of reasoning; it confirms our logic. It shows that our experience in the world supports our reasoning and assertion. When debating, cue yourself to provide evidence by saying "for example."

Relating Assertions, Reasoning, and Evidence

To see the relationship between assertion, reasoning, and evidence, we can use the analogy of a house. Assertion is like the roof, reasoning supports it like the load-bearing walls hold up a roof. Evidence, in turn, is the foundation on which the walls rest.

Below are two examples of how assertion, reasoning, and evidence work together to provide a complete argument.

> I deserve a good grade in this class (*assertion*) because I have worked very hard this year (*reasoning*). For example, I wrote a long research paper and turned all homework in on time (*evidence*).

> Oranges are better than bananas (*assertion*) because oranges are very nutritious (*reasoning*). For example, they have lots of vitamin C and fiber (*evidence*).

SUGGESTED EXERCISES

1. What Is the Reason?

This exercise is designed to develop powerful, impromptu reasoning skills. Please provide the best, most defensible reason for the assertions listed below.

Children should not have cell phones, because . . .

All students should learn a foreign language, because . . .

Parents should not purchase violent video games for their children, because . . .

Schools should review student online behavior, because . . .

The United States should tax carbon, because . . .

Supreme Court justices should have term limits, because . . .

Public colleges should be free for all students, because . . .

The U.S. should have English as the official national language, because . . .

2. What Is the Assertion?

Create an assertion for each of the reasons listed below. Each assertion should be a clear, brief statement of an opinion. For example, for the statement "Because drug use among teenagers is increasing," you might assert: "schools should require drug testing for participation in extracurricular activities."

Because traffic gridlock is a problem,

Because movies targeting teens are too violent,

Because fast-food workers are paid too low a wage,

Because personal privacy on the Internet should be protected,

Because private ownership of handguns protects households,

Because food security is important for health in developing countries,

Because there are too many standardized tests for college admission,

Because it is important to protect journalists' confidential sources,

An Introduction to Evidence

Evidence comes in many forms. It might be expert testimony (including the knowledge and experience of the debater), statistical information from student research, analogies, or hypotheticals.

EXAMPLES

The most basic type of evidence is the example. We can define an example as an occurrence, model, case, or sample that illustrates an issue. On the topic, "The United States should abolish the death penalty," the proposition team might argue that the death penalty should be banned because it might lead to the execution of an innocent person. To support this contention a proposition speaker might argue:

> Kennedy Brewer was released from prison in February 2008 after being cleared of murdering a child. DNA evidence not only proved his innocence but also led to the real killer. Having served 15 years in prison, including time spent on Mississippi's death row, he was freed. He is one of 18 men serving time on death row who have been released due to investigation and legal work by the Innocence Project.

This example supports the speaker's reasoning: the criminal justice system might wrongfully convict and execute an innocent person because a number of innocent men have already been convicted and faced death.

Examples come from a variety of sources—classes, current events, and your own experience. You might use examples from world history or constitutional history and law classes, or you might use one from yesterday's newspaper. You might use the outcome of a policy in one state to project its success in another. For example, a debater might suggest that because health care exchanges were successful in California, they might be successful in other states.

You could also use examples from your personal experience to prove your arguments, although you should be cautious in doing so. Personal examples are generally weak evidence because they are applicable to one individual and may have little meaning for others. Examples are stronger evidence when they can be connected to a larger group of people, a set of circumstances, or to some general principle, idea, or trend. Use your own experience as a starting point, but only rarely as the last word.

You can also use hypothetical examples in a debate. A hypothetical example is fictional but is based on a situation that is understandable and reasonable to a listener. It is conjecture based on known facts. For example, a proposition team arguing in support of the topic, "Junk food should be banned in school." might say:

> A ban on junk food would leave students with only healthy food choices during the school day. Students would prefer to eat something, even a less-desired choice, than go hungry. Consumption of fruit, vegetables, low-fat foods, and non-sugary drinks would increase.

The speaker is imagining what would happen if junk food were banned. Because the ban is not yet in place, he is offering a hypothetical example, a prophecy of student behavior. Hypothetical examples are weaker than other types of example because they have not yet been tested and observed.

Hypothetical examples are particularly valuable in impromptu debating. Because the topic is known only 30 minutes before the opening speech, debaters have little time to prepare. They might not have detailed knowledge of the topic and so may not be able to draw on other types of evidence to support their arguments. In such case, using hypothetical examples might be an option.

Regardless of where you find your example and what type of example you use, you must establish that it is relevant and closely tied to the assertion and reasoning of your argument. To produce examples to prove your reasoning, think:

- When has this circumstance been true in the past?

- What similar situations can I identify in my life or in the life of my community?

- How have those situations worked out?

Work on developing the skill of drawing connections between events so that you can use examples from one situation to apply to another

---

Questions to Ask About Examples

- Is the example general? Can I apply it to other people and situations?

- Does the example support the reasoning? How?

- Are there specific circumstances that make this example true that might not apply in your case? Is it a better example for a different point?

STATISTICS

Statistics are another popular and powerful type of evidence. Statistics are numerical data that tell us something about a group of people or a set of actions or objects. For example, a public opinion poll will tell us what people are thinking about a controversial political issue; business marketing research will tell a company how people perceive their product.

Statistical information can be divided into two categories: generalizable and specific. Generalizable statistical information refers to commonly known data, such as the population of the planet. Because generalizable statistics are well-known, the judge and audience will view this information as reliable. Other statistical information is taken from specific research. A debater must identify a credible source of information (author, report title, publication, date) to establish the trustworthiness of this data. Specific research might include the number of minimum wage workers in the United States (available from the Bureau of Labor Statistics) or the number of annual preventable deaths from air pollution in China (found in the "2010 Global Burden of Disease Study").

You can use statistical information to imply that a particular condition or fact exists. For example, if you could prove that 50% of American high school students cannot find Montana on a map, you might use this to prove that our existing methods for teaching geography are failing. Or, if you could demonstrate that 70% of the rivers in the United States are significantly polluted, you might use this information to argue that the United States needs to clean up its rivers.

Statistics rarely represent the opinions of the overwhelming majority of people, at least not directly. Statisticians collect data by sampling, that is, reviewing data from a select number of people who are deemed to be representative of the larger population and drawing a conclusion based on the opinion of that group. For example, in June 2013, the Gallup organization, a major U.S. consulting and polling company, reported that Congress had a 10 percent approval rating, one of the lowest approval percentages for any institution that Gallup had evaluated in 40 years. That result was not based on investigating the opinions of hundreds of millions of Americans. The poll only directly revealed the opinions of those individuals surveyed by Gallup, in this case a sampling of 1,529 adults, aged 18 and older, living in all 50 U.S. states and the District of Columbia. Statisticians carefully evaluate samples to reach their conclusions, but the methodology of any survey is subject to evaluation, criticism, and challenge by other survey evidence in a debate. Statistics are not 100 percent accurate, which is why reputable polls include a margin of error, the measure of accuracy of the results. In the case of the survey above, Gallup cautioned that the maximum margin of sampling error is +/– 3 percentage points.

Like any other kind of evidence, statistical samples need to be representative of the issue you are discussing. Remember that one problem with using personal examples is that what is true for you may not be true for another person. Similarly, what is true for one group of people may not be true of another group. In debates, however, you cannot simply say: "We don't know if this is true for everyone." You must actually counter with some evidence of your own or provide a clear and convincing reason why the evidence is unlikely to be representative of the larger issue.

Evidence makes a complete argument but the presence of evidence is not sufficient to prove a point in a debate. Evidence may be refuted. Evidence may be challenged based on the source of material, the perceived bias of the source, the timeliness of the information, the method of analysis, the application of the information for argumentation, and the consistency of the information when tested by other authorities. We'll examine the methods of challenging evidence in the next chapter.

SUGGESTED EXERCISES

1. Complete the Argument—A-R-E

The table below includes some assertions, reasoning, and evidence for an argument. Fill in the missing information to make complete arguments.

A (Assertion)	R (Reasoning)	E (Evidence)
1. The voting age should be lowered to 16.	Younger citizens are excluded from important decisions—those about health and education policy, for example, that matter a great deal to them.	

2.		By the time a child is 18, she will have witnessed 16,000 murders on television.
3. The United States should abolish the death penalty.		
4.		UN inspectors operating in Iran have reported that Iran has slowed its collection of uranium, an element required to make a nuclear weapon.
5. Edward Snowden should be prosecuted for releasing classified material.	Classified documents protect the identity of intelligence staff and contacts, who might be at risk if their identities are revealed.	
6. The police should be permitted to gather DNA evidence and use it for investigations.	DNA evidence can be used to identify criminals and solve cold cases.	
7. Schools should not participate in animal dissection in classes.		

2. Offering Evidence

Complete the argument by offering evidence for the following statements:

- Political candidates do not follow their campaign promises when they are elected to office. For example,

- Individuals eat the wrong foods and that promotes obesity. For example,

- Schools restrict student speech too severely. For example,

- The United States is needed to police violence in other parts of the world. For example,

- People do not appreciate their U.S. citizenship as much as they did in the past. For example,

- There are times when it is a moral duty to break the law. For example,

- There are unintended consequences to public policy change. For example,

Thinking Critically About Advertisements

Because you will make and critically evaluate arguments during a debate, you must understand what makes a strong—or weak—argument. One way to do so is to analyze the arguments embedded in advertising.

Most advertising is a form of argument. There is an assertion: "Shop this weekend at our special holiday sale!" There is reasoning: "Great values are available on all clothing for women and children." There is evidence to support the reasoning: "At least 20% off all items and up to 60% off retail prices. Additional markdowns on summer closeouts!"

Advertising does not always include all A-R-E elements. In many cases, the reasoning or evidence is implied. For example, you might see an advertisement for Lustrous shampoo showing a young woman with unbelievably shiny hair surrounded by a large group of adoring friends. Underneath the picture is the slogan "Lustrous—Simply the Best." What are you supposed to reason from the ad? You are expected to conclude that she has attracted so many friends *because* her hair is so shiny and that her hair is so lovely *because* of Lustrous. Therefore, you should buy Lustrous shampoo. Let's look at how this works in reverse, and you'll see the familiar **A-R-E** pattern:

Assertion: You need Lustrous shampoo.

Reasoning: (Because) Using this shampoo will get you lots of friends.

Evidence: This girl has used the shampoo and she has lots of friends.

This advertisement offers implied reasoning and evidence. This may not be *good* reasoning and evidence, but it is still reasoning and evidence.

Remember that advertisements are trying to get you to spend money on a product. One response to these demands is to surrender your money. Another is to critically question advertisements' claims. Consider this advertising claim: "Twenty-five of the people we asked preferred the new Tip-Top peanut butter." Thinking critically about the claim, you might ask the following questions before you purchase the product:

- What was the basis for the preference—taste, availability, aesthetics, cost?

- Preferred to what other choice?

- How many people were asked?

- What is the percentage of positive respondents? Are 25 respondents 2% of those who preferred the brand or 75%?

Finding the answers to these kinds of questions will enable you to decide if the advertiser has made a strong or weak argument or if you need more information before you decide on whether the product is for you.

1. Advertising Analysis

Develop three or more questions that you would want answered about each of the following advertising claims:

- This is the best price that you will get on mattresses this season.

- This is your last chance to get the sport edition of this vehicle. Hurry in before they are all gone!

- This is the only antiperspirant activated by motion.

2. Find the A-R-E in Advertising

Choose four different advertisements—two from print sources and two from television or the Internet. Find the assertion, reasoning, and evidence in the advertisement. Consider if any of the three parts of an argument might be hidden or embedded in the ad. Determine whether the advertisement makes a strong argument, a weak argument, or if you don't have enough information to decide.

CHAPTER 5:
REFUTATION

Since debating requires a clash of ideas, you cannot win debates simply by making arguments for your side. You must challenge and undermine your opponent's arguments while defending your own. Debaters call this skill "refutation." Refutation exposes the flaws in an opponent's argument and proves that it is false or that it fails to offer support for his position while showing that your arguments are superior.

Goal of Refutation

The goal of all refutation is to prove that your team's arguments are superior to those of the other side. In fact, the ideal position is to argue that any one of your arguments is better than the sum of arguments for the other team.

You establish the superiority of your arguments by showing that they are:

- better reasoned.

- based on more credible sources of information.

- based on less-biased sources of information.

- based on more recent events or sources of information.

- more empirically sound—they are based on statistical information, case studies, historical examples, contemporary examples, expert opinions, and analogies.

- consistent over time and in different locations.

- more typical and representative.

- consensus or majority opinions.

- account for contrary opinions presented by the other team.

Strategies for Refutation

During refutation, you not only explain why your arguments are superior but also why your opponent's ideas are weak or wrong. You can do so using three strategies:

- **Choose to Account or Answer:** Using this strategy, you first must decide if the argument should be answered or ignored. Not every idea deserves a reply. Ideas can be repetitious, trivial, or irrelevant. Don't spend time replying to weak and insignificant arguments. Analyze your opponent's arguments and answer only the genuinely powerful ones.

  If you think an argument does not deserve a reply, you cannot simply ignore it, however. You must "account" for it, that is, explain why an argument does not deserve an answer. For example, a debater might say:

  > My opponents have presented four issues in the debate. But the first, second, and third all make the same point. (*Explain why the first three arguments make the same point.*) I will answer the first argument and the fourth. Answering the first will take care of arguments two and three.

  If you simply ignore an argument, the judge might think you have conceded it and give credit to your opponent for winning the point.

- **Use Direct and Indirect Refutation:** You can also use direct and indirect refutation to challenge an opponent's arguments. Direct refutation challenges the reasoning and evidence supporting the specific arguments made by the opposing team. For example, in a debate on "The United States should substantially declassify national security secrets," the first proposition speaker might present a case supporting declassification, perhaps arguing that more open government would promote democracy and avoid foreign policy mistakes. Using direct refutation, the opposition would contest the proposition's arguments, showing that open government would not benefit democracy or prevent foreign policy missteps.

Directly refuting a case can be difficult, however, because you are challenging your opponent on his own ground. In developing the case, your opponents have selected the strongest arguments and best evidence they can find. Refuting these arguments may be impossible. In that case, utilize indirect refutation.

Indirect refutation involves presenting any relevant argument that is not specific to the opposing team's previously stated position. It offers new material that adds to your team's position. For example, in the debate over declassification above, the opposition could argue that declassifying secrets might promote democracy, but it would also hurt national security and threaten people's lives. This argument is relevant to the case but unrelated to the two arguments the proposition has presented. Because indirect refutation can introduce significant new ideas into the debate, it is usually more effective than challenging reasoning and evidence through direct refutation.

- **Use Strategic Agreement:** You do not have to disagree with an argument to refute it. You can agree with an opponent and still effectively undermine his argument by using what is known as "strategic agreement." To do so, you would acknowledge that an argument is legitimate but assert that it actually works against your opponent's interests. You can do so using three approaches:

    1. *Argument agreement to develop a different and better argument.* Using this approach, you would agree with the underlying premise

of your opponent's argument but then use it to develop a different argument. When debating the topic "The United States should significantly improve traffic safety regulations," for example, a proposition team might support the adoption of traffic safety laws that require cars to have a brake override to stop runaway cars and to have sensors that prevent them from starting unless all passengers have fastened their seatbelts. The opposition might *agree* that the laws would guarantee that new safety features would be added to cars, but then present a different idea: more safety regulations would increase the number of accidents. The new safety features would give drivers a false sense of security and, therefore, drivers might be willing to take more risks—which would result in more accidents and deaths.

2. *Argument agreement as* reductio ad absurdum. Using *reductio ad absurdum* (reduction to the absurd), you would demonstrate that an argument is false by extending it to the point of absurdity. In 1729, Jonathan Swift made such an argument in a satirical essay about British policies in Ireland, which had resulted in misery and starvation throughout the country. In "A Modest Proposal for Preventing the Children of Poor People in Ireland from Being a Burden to their Parents or Country, and for Making them Beneficial to the Public," he used the theories underlying British policies to argue that the impoverished Irish might ease their economic problems by fattening up their children and selling them as food for the rich.

3. *Turn or Capture an Opponent's Argument.* Using this strategy, you would agree with your opponent's argument and then turn it against him, showing that actually becomes a reason to vote for you. For example, your opponent might argue: Freedom of expression is dangerous because everyone can then make racist comments that can cause all sorts of conflicts. You would offer a counterargument: The expression of racist comments and the subsequent conflict brings issues to light—the comments can be exposed and countered, improving social safety and security. In this way, the interests of victims of racism can be protected.

Refutation Thinking Method

The Four-Step Method of Refutation is a thinking exercise that trains debaters in refutation. Using this method, the debater identifies the opponent's argument, imagines that it is wrong, analyzes the issue and develops evidence to explain why the argument is wrong, and, finally, reaches a conclusion that explains why proving that the argument is wrong matters.

Almost all refutation can follow this method:

Step 1: They say: Reference the specific argument you are about to refute *so that your opponent and the judge can identify the issue and follow your* argument. Don't generalize your opponent's position. Debating involves the careful and nuanced development of arguments, so use your opponent's words.

Step 2: But they are wrong: This is a valuable critical thinking component of the refutation. Begin by assuming that your opponent's reasoning and evidence are wrong. Then work to identify what might be wrong.

Step 3: Because: This is the argumentation stage of the method. To disagree, you must make a complete argument in reply. Your opponent is wrong [claim] because . . . [of an opposing reasoned and evidenced position].

Step 4: Therefore: Conclude by comparing your refutation to your opponent's argument and showing why your point defeats his. You can do this by evaluating his argument's relevance, reasoning, evidence, and significance.

Let's see how the method would work to criticize a debate argument based on the health care cost savings of the Affordable Care Act:

[They say] Our opponents argued that the Affordable Care Act, also known as Obamacare, would lower health care costs in the United States.

[But they are wrong] That is not accurate—it will increase costs.

[Because] There are not enough cost controls in the legislation. Insurance companies are not reducing costs—individual premiums and deductibles are increasing. Massachusetts was the model for Obamacare. According to a 2013 report of the Massachusetts-based Center for Health Information and Analysis, health insurance deductibles in Massachusetts surged by more than 40 percent between 2009 and 2011, a period when health benefits were reduced by 5 percent and premiums rose by nearly 10 percent

[Therefore] The Affordable Care Act will not be affordable in the long term. Benefits will be cut and Americans will incur higher health care costs and receive less comprehensive and lower-quality care.

As you learn to debate, use the verbal cues for each step of the method when organizing and presenting your arguments during preparation and practice. It will help you remember to apply all of the parts of the method to your response. Later, when you are more experienced, you should be able to drop these prompts as you will remember to use all the parts.

Using this method compels you to carefully analyze another person's arguments. It encourages you to be thoughtful and engaging when listening to someone's opinions. Of course, you can use the method in debates, but you can also use it to analyze opinions of family and friends, in the classroom and other extracurricular activities, and while listening to news reports, politicians, and experts. Employing this procedure increases your chances of accepting legitimate opinions and avoiding being manipulated. If you follow these steps and can't find anything wrong with an opinion, you might want to adopt it or share it with others.

1. Practice Direct Refutation

Select a series of debate topics or arguments from the list below and develop direct refutation using the Four-Step Method of Refutation.

- Governments should collect DNA samples from arrested persons.

- Student bystanders should be punished for failing to stop bullying.

- Schools should not block online access to personal and social media sites.

- Governments should be able to shut down the Internet.

- Private school loans should be dischargeable in bankruptcy.

- The U.S. Supreme Court should televise its proceedings.

- Hydrofracking does more good than harm.

- States should require drug tests to receive welfare benefits.

- Students should be allowed to carry registered guns on university campuses.

- Political advertising does more good than harm.

2. Practice the Four-Step Method of Refutation

Ask each member of your group to write an assertion on a slip of paper and put it in a pile at the front of the room. Mix up the slips and have each member choose one. Then have each member use the Four-Step Method to refute the assertion.

Effective Refutation

Effective refutation begins with argument anticipation, the process a debater uses to imagine an opponent's possible challenges to her arguments. If a debater can determine her opponent's potential replies, she will be in a better position to craft stronger arguments. She will also be able to adapt her arguments to avoid, minimize, or overwhelm any criticisms. When anticipating an argument:

- **Imagine your argument:** "X."

- **Anticipate your opponent's response:** What will he say when I argue X?

- **Consider your argument again:** How will I respond to his criticisms?

- **Continue the process:** What will he say in response to my reply? What will I say then?

Following this procedure will help you select an argument that is more likely to be a winning position. You have considered what your opponent might argue and know that your position is a winning one *before* introducing the argument in you speech.

REFUTATION SCALE

In addition to argument anticipation, you should refute opposing arguments based on the Refutation Scale below. This scale describes four refutation tactics ranked in order of efficiency. The first tactic takes the least amount of time in a speech, the last tactic requires the most effort. All the tactics are effective and you might use one or several to reply to a single opposing argument.

Refutation Scale

1. Relevance

2. Significance

3. Turn/Capture

4. Answer

1. **Relevance.** Explain that the argument is not relevant to the topic of the debate. It is off topic; it misses the point. Because it doesn't address the issues germane to the debate, the judge shouldn't consider it.

2. **Significance.** Explain how your argument is more important than the opposition's. An argument could be either more qualitatively or quantitatively significant, or both.

3. **Turn/Capture.** Turn your opponent's argument and use it against him. *Turn* is an abbreviation of the expression "turning the tables," a reversing of position. For example, an opponent might criticize a speaker for supporting policies that increase the federal deficit. The speaker might reply that the opponent is supporting positions that would even more greatly increase the deficit. If "increasing the deficit" is bad, then the argument applies more to the other side.

   Turns can be either link turns or significance turns. A link is a causal connection; it makes the point that A is connected to B. In a debate, this connection would be explained in an argument's reasoning and evidence. A link turn demonstrates that a cause, or argument, link is reversed. For example, in a debate on the topic "The United States should end economic sanctions," the proposition might argue:

Sanctions should end because trade and aid restrictions ultimately hurt only the poor. Government officials do not suffer from the economic hardships brought on by sanctions: the leadership protects its own economic position. Restrictions on goods and services and higher prices are felt by and hurt the poor and socially marginalized groups.

The argument makes the causal connection or link:

Economic sanctions $\longrightarrow$ Hardship for the poor

The opposition might try to turn the link for this argument, the causal claim that economic sanctions hurt the poor, by arguing that ending economic sanctions would produce more misery for the poor:

Ending sanctions will open markets to multinational companies and foreign investment; money will flow to the politically well-connected and their income and opportunities will increase dramatically relative to those of poor and socially marginalized groups. Government leaders will make economic and social decisions to benefit from this unequal distribution of wealth. These changes in the economy will not benefit the poor and their hardships will actually increase.

Ending economic sanctions $\longrightarrow$ More hardship for the poor

A significance turn is an argument that reverses the claims associated with an argument's significance or outcome. On the topic "The United States should end economic sanctions," the proposition team has argued that "sanctions hurt the poor in the sanctioned countries. Economic consequences include unemployment and hunger." The opposition might argue that these are not exclusively negative consequences, that there might be a "silver lining":

Although there might be hardship in the short term, economic sanctions will not produce substantial increases in morbidity or mortality. People will struggle, but they will not be sicker or die. They will recognize their callous treatment by the government, however, and protest their government's policies, putting pressure on their leadership to reform and have more equal distribution of economic benefits, as well as better protect human rights. If the conditions for the poor are severe, they will rise up and force the government to reform, encouraging the country to change leadership and make a transition to a more inclusive political system.

In this case, the opposition team is taking the position that "hardship for the poor" might have more benefits than costs.

Prop: Hardship for the poor ⟶ Opp: Hardship for the poor can promote reform

The opposition team has reversed the proposition's significance argument: that which was "bad" is now "good."

You can also capture an opponent's argument. For example, an opponent might argue that his team's position would help protect the rights of criminal defendants. A speaker refuting this point might argue that her team's position offers even better protection for the same group. The speaker would capture the argument from her opponent.

4. **Answer.** If an idea is relevant and has significance that cannot be minimized, and you are unable to turn or capture it, then you must refute it by answering it. In doing so, remember to carefully assess your opponent's points: Are they complete arguments? Are they weak? Are they important? Do they matter to a large number of people?

Traps in Refutation

Debaters must employ sophisticated techniques when refuting, but they must also avoid two traps of conventional, and often ineffective, refutation.

- **The "X, -X" Problem.** Refuting an o-pponent's argument by arguing the opposite position is a good tactic, but all too frequently this produces the "X, -X" problem. Imagine an argument with the value, "X." The opposite of this argument has the value of "-X." Let's use your math skills and place the arguments in an equation: $X + (-X)$. What is the result? Zero. For example:

  Proposition speaker: Tax increases will slow economic growth

  Opposition speaker: No, more taxes will promote economic growth.

  In this case, a debater has argued an issue and her opponent has argued the opposite, so neither side wins the point. Often debaters will continue repeating this tactic, but that does not help improve their chance of success. The result of $X + (-X) + X + (-X) + X + (-X)$ is still "0."

- **The "X Y" Problem.** Arguing your own "talking points" and failing to consider the issues your opponent has raised is also an error. Imagine that the opening proposition speaker makes an argument with value "X." Her opponent chooses a different argument in support of his side of the debate and argues in favor of that argument "Y." For example:

  Proposition speaker: Tax increases will improve economic growth. (X)

  Opposition speaker: An infrastructure bank will improve economic growth. (Y)

  Each side then continues to present their argument to the end of the debate without addressing their opponent's. The arguments are like two ships passing in the night. The judge has no basis for comparing arguments or knowing which is better.

Making Refutation Choices

Making appropriate refutation choices is not a simple decision, but keeping the following in mind will help you:

- Use the Four-Step Method of Refutation.

- Avoid the "X, –X" Problem.

- Avoid the "X Y" Problem.

- Choose to Account or Reply/Answer.

- Use Direct Refutation and Indirect Refutation.

- Utilize Strategic Agreement.

Using Refutation

Refutation should occur early, often, and powerfully. Both sides of a debate should use every opportunity to attain a psychological edge with the judge—a proof that their team is the best in the debate. A clever team tries to convince the judge that it has won the contest in one of their early speeches. They try to make clear that there is no debate. They are so far ahead of their opponents that no reasonable person would consider the event to be a debate because it is too one-sided.

CHAPTER 6:

HECKLING AND POINTS OF INFORMATION

Debates are more engaging and challenging for participants and the audience if they include dynamic elements. The Public Debate Program encourages debaters to use two of these: argumentative heckling and points of information (POI). Points of information and heckling encourage impromptu argumentation and make the debate exciting, interactive, and fun. In the hands of skilled debaters, they are also important strategic tools.

Heckling

Heckling refers to an expression that interrupts or intrudes on another person's speech. Most people think of heckling as jeering, booing, hissing, or shouting negative comments to the speaker. This is disruptive heckling, also known as "barracking," and is not permitted in PDP debates. Argumentative heckling, on the other hand, is a form of dynamic and spontaneous response to a speaker's presentation. It is directed not to the speaker but to the judge in an effort to persuade her of the brilliance of a speaker's point or to show displeasure with an opponent's opinion. Heckling is a part of a team's strategy; it is a tactic they devise when preparing for a competition.

Heckling allows debaters to continue to create, develop, and present ideas throughout a debate. It also ensures fairness by permitting the opposition team to communicate with the judge to the end of the debate, after their speaking time and opportunities for points of information have ended (remember, the proposition has the last speech). Finally, it adds information to assist the judge's deliberations on the key issues when determining the debate's outcome.

Argumentative heckles are:

- relevant, an immediate response based on the precise language and argument of the speaker.

- spoken to the judge and not delivered to the speaker.

- constructive responses that add to the judge's understanding of the debate.

- only 1–2 words, almost never 3. Anything more and a debater is making a speech.

They also include the meaningful elements of argument—reasoning and evidence—in extremely concise or implied form.

Argumentative heckling is minimal, respectful, and on point. It avoids repetition of material that is otherwise included in a team's speeches and is specific to the information in the speech the heckling is addressing. Because heckling is used to persuade the judge, you should consider whether she would welcome a particular heckle before using it.

HECKLING TACTICS

PDP debaters use argumentative heckling for two purposes: to counter an opponent and support their teammates. Debates include communication and miscommunication. Debaters make listening and note recording errors, have issues of clarity, misinterpret statements and need clarifications, and introduce suspect fact claims. Heckling allows participants to revise a debate's history in an appropriate way. Heckling can also be a sign of respect for teammates and opponents and can be used to show agreement with a specific point the speaker has made.

Heckling

Use heckling to:

- Announce rules violations

- Identify argument fallacies

- Reveal contradictions

- Expose incomplete ideas

- Correct errors

- Introduce counterexamples

- Support teammates

Heckling to Counter an Opponent

Argumentative heckling provides an opportunity for teams to undermine the substance of an opposing idea, as well as correct errors. You can use heckling to:

- **Announce rules violations.** Most PDP rules are easy to understand, but some are difficult to apply. For example, speakers may not introduce new arguments in the rebuttal speeches, but determining if an argument is new may be difficult. To a rebuttal speaker, an issue may have its foundation in a teammate's earlier speech. To an opponent, the same issue may sound like an entirely new one. For the opponent, an effective technique to counter the presentation of new material is to heckle. In fact, heckling may be the only option available. If the speech is the proposition rebuttal, the opposition team does not have any formal speaking time left. The opposition has finished all three of its team's speeches and points of information are not permitted during the short rebuttal speeches. Heckling is the only way to announce a disagreement with the proposition side.

A quick heckle, "New!" is sufficient to announce a rules violation. It is an argument. The reasoning for the heckle is known to all participants from the rules—the rules allow no new arguments in rebuttal speeches. The evidence is from the voice of the speaker. Whatever it was that the speaker had just said is the *empirical proof* that it was a new argument. In addition, this heckle is brief, just a single word. It is not disruptive. It is directed to the judge.

The speaker is likely to dismiss the heckle, but it might matter a great deal to the judge. If the judge considers the argument to be new, she won't give it any weight during her deliberation. In other words, this particular heckle is telling the judge to ignore the speaker's argument. If successful, that is quite a lot to accomplish with a single word spoken during an opponent's speech.

- **Identify argument fallacies.** Debates center around arguments, some of which inevitably will include errors known as "argument fallacies." You can use heckling to identify them. For example, a speaker in a debate on the topic "Free speech should protect hate speech" might say "The United States should continue to provide First Amendment protection for hate speech. This has been done in the past and ought to be done now." The fact that something has been done does not mean that it is a correct or better behavior. The speaker appears to be committing the fallacy of appeal to tradition. An opponent might heckle by saying "Tradition!" or "Fallacy—Tradition!" The heckle may be effective because it undermines the speaker's argument or because it forces the speaker to work harder to successfully make the argument than if no heckle had been made.

- **Reveal contradictions.** As the speakers and arguments increase over the course of a debate, teams are likely to offer contradictory or inconsistent arguments. You can alert the judge to these by heckling.

On the topic, "The United States should abolish the death penalty," for example, the first proposition speaker might claim that the death penalty should be abolished because it is used so infrequently and inconsistently that it does not deter murderers. The second proposition speaker might add the argument that the death penalty is likely to kill an innocent person because U.S. states are sentencing so many people to death that it is inevitable that an innocent person will be executed.

The opposition team would then identify the contradiction. The opening proposition speaker argued that the death penalty was ineffective in deterring crime because it was rarely used. But the second proposition speaker argued that the death penalty might be applied to an innocent person because it was used frequently. In this case the opposition might heckle: "Contradiction on use" or "Used or not?" or "Contradicts deterrence." These heckles let the judge know what to look for and encourages her to act like a member of the opposition team, analyzing the proposition team's arguments to find error.

- **Expose incomplete ideas.** Heckling can expose incomplete arguments, those that are mere assertions and lack reasoning and/or evidence. On the topic, "The United States should provide development assistance to Central America," a proposition speaker might argue that the United States should give development aid to Central America to encourage economic growth. The opposition, however, is aware of cases where development assistance has impeded economic growth and produced more costs than benefits. So, after the proposition speaker finishes her analysis, the opposition demands evidence by heckling: "For example?" This heckle reveals that the proposition's issue is not a complete argument.

- **Correct mistaken claims.** You can use a heckle to point out that your opponent's information is false or so distasteful that it never should have been mentioned. For example, in a debate on "The United States should increase gas taxes," a proposition speaker might argue that the United States should increase gas taxes because doing so will encourage the energy industry to turn to renewable sources. Doing so would produce more jobs in the energy sector and job growth is good for the economy. An opposition speaker might reply that more jobs are at risk if gas prices increased than could ever be gained in turning to renewable energy because more workers are needed to produce gas energy than renewable energy, thus the United States would suffer a net job loss. If job growth is needed, then gas taxes are a bad idea.

Now, let's imagine that the opposition does not argue this point further and that the third proposition speaker then makes the following point:

> In our opening speech, our team established that we need gas tax increases to encourage the development of renewable energy. Why? Because that will produce more jobs. And our opponents have ignored that issue for the entire debate.

But the opposition did not ignore the issue! The proposition team misrepresented what had happened in the debate and did so in the last speech—when the opposition had no more speech time and no opportunities for points of information. The only way to correct the distortion is with a heckle, "Shame!" "Shame!" reveals that the proposition seriously objects to what is being said. Once again, the heckle is directed to the judge. You are communicating that your opponent's claim is so wrong that it should not be part of the debate. The heckle calls on the judge to identify when and how the argument was introduced because it is wrong to claim that the opposition team overlooked the argument.

This heckle must be used cautiously to avoid it becoming a disruptive heckle. Do not use it to show general disagreement with an opponent. Everyone knows the two teams disagree—that's the point of a debate! "Shame!" is best used to correct mistaken claims by the other team.

- **Introduce counterexamples.** In debate argumentation, evidence is used to support a speaker's reasoning. You can disprove that reasoning by using a heckle to offer a counterexample. For example, let's suppose that a proposition speaker debating "Nuclear weapons do more good than harm" has argued that nuclear weapons helped promote international stability during the Cold War because they produced a military stalemate between the United States and the Soviet Union. Each country had enough nuclear weapons to destoy the other. But then the speaker went too far. He asserted that the possession of nuclear weapons could prevent conflict and concluded by claiming that nuclear weapons had never been used in a conflict. His opponent heckled "Hiroshima!," an effective counterexample.

This heckle was effective because it did not merely reply to the speaker. It also reinforced an argument the opposition team had made: nuclear proliferation increased the likelihood of conflict if one country had nuclear weapons and its enemy did not. Mutually assured destruction led to peace because both countries possessed large numbers of nuclear weapons. But if one country has a nuclear weapon and the other does not, then nuclear weapon possession might lead to the use of the weapon. The Hiroshima heckle effectively countered the speaker and, at the same time, supported another of the team's arguments. This is an excellent heckled counterexample.

Heckling to Support Teammates

Argumentative heckling is also a valuable tactic to show support. For example, applause is a form of heckling that is used to support debaters in two ways. All those attending PDP debates—debaters, judges, coaches, teachers, timekeepers, and audience members—applaud at the beginning and the end of each debater's speech. Applause welcomes a speaker to the front of a room before she begins her speech and thanks her for her effort when she has finished.

Teammates may also use applause to support each other's key arguments. They do not do this to show general support; everyone knows that teammates support one another. Instead, they select one or more key issues that might alter the outcome of the debate and applaud those.

The applause signals the judge to *pay careful attention* to the speaker's arguments.

The PDP applause tradition encourages participants and audiences to pound or rap on a desk or tabletop with knuckles or open palm, knocking or slapping a hand three or four times.

PREVENTING AND REPLYING TO HECKLES

Speakers should anticipate that opponents will heckle and so should prepare to answer them. You can reduce the likelihood of heckling by delivering complete and detailed arguments that you can back up with further evidence and reasoning if challenged. Simply put, good debating reduces heckling.

The speaker has two advantages in replying to heckles. First, because she replies *after* the heckle, she has a psychological advantage. If she is able to give an effective reply, she appears to have "won" the point raised by the heckle. Second, the reply is not restricted in the same way a heckle is. Argumentative heckles are very brief—1 or 2 words—but the speaker's response may be detailed and she may use as much time as she chooses. It is, therefore, difficult for heckles to undermine prepared or experienced opponents. Argumentative heckles can distract an opponent and limit the speaker's overall effectiveness, however, because they take time away from a speaker's effective reply to another argument.

Try to anticipate heckles and prepare a counter-heckle. For example, in reply to the heckle, "Shame!" the speaker usually tries to capture the power of the word and use it against the heckler by answering, "Yes, it is a shame that my opponent does not understand this point . . . " or "Yes, it is a shame that thousands of people are victimized by policies supported by my opponents. . . . " The speaker continues with her argument and simply includes the word *shame* as part of it.

Other counter-heckles you can use include:

"Fascinating, and irrelevant."

"Yes, we all heard that the first time."

"There you go again."

"You seem to be stuck on an idea that has already been answered."

"Already answered."

"I'm getting to that. Please be patient."

You can't use these counter-heckles and then say nothing more about the heckle. These counters are opening remarks in your reply to the heckle. You must have at least another sentence or two explaining your counter idea. For example, after countering a heckle with "Fascinating, and irrelevant," a speaker then explains how the heckle is irrelevant. It is not effective for a debater to reply, "Yes, we all heard that the first time," unless she can show that the heckle or the argument it supported was made and defeated earlier in the debate. Don't remind a judge that you already heard a heckle if you or your teammates have never addressed it.

AUDIENCE HECKLING

PDP debates permit audience heckling. Audiences should applaud all debaters as they begin and end their speeches and may also applaud outstanding arguments offered by speakers from both sides. The audience should not support a particular side nor should they engage in argumentative heckling as if they were part of one of the teams in a debate. And, of course, they are not permitted to barrack or use disruptive heckling.

When the noise from heckling temporarily interferes with a judge's ability to hear what a speaker is saying, the judge will simply rap or knock on a desktop and call out, "Order! Order!" That signal is a reminder that the noise level is rising and behavior is getting a bit out of hand. A call for order does not ban heckling for the remainder of a debate—it is a request to pay attention to what is going on,

Points of Information

A point of information (POI) is a request by a speaker's opponent to yield speaking time for the opponent to make an argument or comment or ask a question. Experienced debaters use POIs much more for argument (often a counterexample) than a question.

The speaker may accept or reject a POI. If the speaker accepts it, the opposing team's point may not last longer than 15 seconds. The speaker accepts only one point at a time. The person making a POI may not interrupt the speaker's answer, ask a two-part or follow-up question, or make any other comment unless the speaker agrees to it by accepting another POI. In accepting a POI, the speaker is not agreeing to anything more than giving up her time.

Why would the speaker give some of her valuable time to the other side? Two reasons. First, speakers want to make their own POIs. If a debater never accepts any points of information, the other team will not accept POIs from him or his team. Second, judges will deduct individual score points from speakers who do not accept POIs. A debater refusing all POIs appears unprepared or unsure of her own arguments. Accepting POIs lets the judge know that the debaters are capable and confident.

More than one member of a team may request a point of information at the same time. In fact, all three members of a team might rise simultaneously for a POI. Each debater should make several requests during unprotected time. Experienced teams might make 12–18 or more requests during their opponents' two constructive speeches.

PROTECTED TIME

Points of information can be requested after the opening minute and before the final minute of the first four (constructive) speeches of a PDP debate. The opening and closing minute of each constructive speech is "protected" so that the speaker gets the full minute to introduce and conclude her speech without major interruptions or distractions. POIs are not permitted during the final (rebuttal) speech for each team.

The speech time for a POI counts against the speaker's time. If the speaker accepts the point, the 6-minute countdown clock will continue to run. If the point is made in 15 seconds and the speaker answers for 15 seconds, she has 4 minutes and 30 seconds remaining in her speech.

A timekeeper or judge signals that the opening minute of a constructive speech has been completed, usually by slapping the palm of her hand one time on a desktop or tabletop. This announces to the debaters that POIs are now permitted. She does the same when 1 minute is left in each speech. With the second sound, debaters know that protected time has started and no POIs may be made for the rest of the speech.

REQUESTING A POINT OF INFORMATION

To request a POI, rise. That's it. Do not speak. If the speaker does not accept your request, sit down immediately. If he denies repeated requests for POIs, you can hold out your hand, almost as if begging him to accept a point. Other gestures are not necessary and may be counterproductive. If a speaker has rejected all POIs and protected time is approaching, you can request a point by saying "Information." You might also use a verbal request if the speaker cannot see you. Verbal requests are not common, however, and are generally considered inappropriate. Constant verbal requests are a form of disruptive heckling. It is non-argumentative noise during an opponent's speech, and judges will treat it as they would barracking.

If your opponent accepts your POI, you have a maximum of 15 seconds to make it. Quickly glance at the speaker as you begin, but direct your point to the judge, who is the one who is deciding the outcome of the debate. When making your point, be polite and persuasive. Don't berate your opponent. You are simply using your opponent's time to communicate an issue to the judge. Once you've made your point, sit down; don't stand to await the speaker's reply. The rules forbid follow-up statements or questions.

REPLYING TO A POINT OF INFORMATION REQUEST

You may accept or reject a point of information. To accept a POI, simply say, "Yes" or "I'll take your point." If more than one member of the opposing team rises to request a point, identify the person whose request you will take. For example, "I will accept the first opposition speaker's point."

You can reject a POI either with a nonverbal gesture or a verbal reply. To request your opponent sit, gently shake your hand down once or twice, in much the same manner a performer gestures the audience to take their seats after an ovation. You could also say "No, thank you" and continue your speech. The nonverbal gesture is preferable because it doesn't interrupt the presentation. Refusing a POI is not considered rude. You have the right to deliver your speech and accept POIs when you think appropriate.

Once you have accepted a POI, determine if it is meaningful or irrelevant before you reply. If the point is meaningful and directed to your ideas, reply briefly, addressing your reply to the judge. Spend enough time addressing the POI to defeat it, but remember that replying should not interfere with your primary goal, delivering an effective, winning speech. Once you have replied, immediately get back to your speech. You do not need to say "Now, back to my speech" or "I would like to get back to my argument." It should be clear that you have answered the point and that you are free to continue your speech as if the point did not happen or no longer mattered.

If you decide the point is irrelevant just get back to your speech, trusting that everyone understood that the point did not connect with the arguments in the debate. Or you respond with: "Just not relevant," or "That misses the point," or "That was interesting. Now back to the debate."

The PDP format has no rule about the number of points you may accept, but if you accept none, you create the impression that you don't trust your arguments or are fearful of criticism. If you accept too many, you may lose control of the organization of your speech or become too distracted to properly construct your own ideas and answer opposing arguments. PDP's individual scoring rubric encourages debaters to accept two POIs and, perhaps, one or two additional points if there is time and doing so does not disrupt your speech.

The Point of Information Process

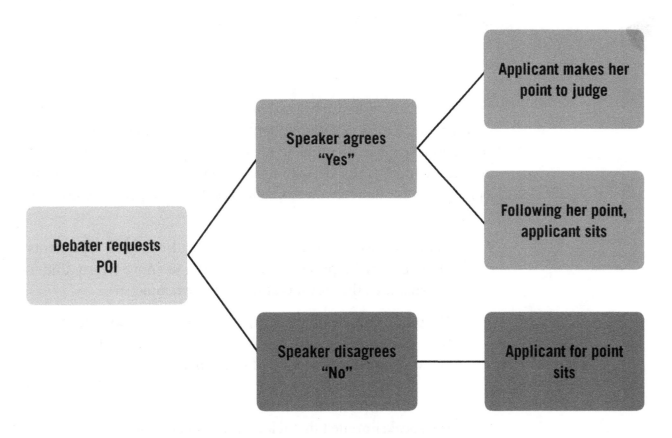

TACTICAL USES OF POINTS OF INFORMATION

Using POIs

Use POIs to

- Understand issues

- Clarify differences

- Evaluate evidence

- Advance arguments

- Attack arguments

Points of information can be used in many of the same ways as heckles —to announce rules violations, identify argument fallacies, reveal contradictions, expose incomplete ideas, correct errors, and introduce counterexamples; the POI, with its 15 seconds speaking time, offers an opportunity for more involved challenges. POIs are generally used for five purposes:

- **Understand issues.** Because debates entail complex arguments, debaters can make points of information to more clearly understand what the other team is arguing. For example:

    The proposition team said that you think it is a good idea for the United States to arm the Syrian rebels. Which rebels will get weapons and what kind of weapons?

    or

    The speaker argued that television is a bad influence on children. Which TV programs is she describing, all television programs, including news programs or award-winning children's programming like *Sesame Street*?

In these examples, knowing more precisely what the opposing team is arguing will be helpful in organizing effective answers.

- **Clarify Differences.** Not every argument in a debate is a point of contention. Opponents may agree on many points. You can use POIs to clarify the arguments on which you and your opponents concur and differ. For example, in the topic "Schools should have uniforms," a debater might use a POI to determine whether both teams agree on the issue of clothing cost: Would you agree school uniforms are less expensive than other clothing choices? Using a POI in this case clarifies the debate for the judge and lets all those involved focus attention on the few important issues that will settle the outcome of the debate

- **Evaluate Evidence.** Debaters sometimes inadvertently introduce errors into a debate. POIs enable you to challenge and correct these. In some cases the error is simple. For example:

  There are only nine members of the U.S. Supreme Court. The arguments about the problem of tie votes by the Court assumes ten, not nine members.

  For many issues, however, the facts are not so clear or do not support just one side of a debate. Points of information can evaluate the evidence, testing it for the quality of the source, whether the information is up-to-date, and the way facts and examples are used to support argumentation.

- **Advance Arguments.** You can use POIs to make arguments supporting your side or to set up a future argument. For example, in a debate on a topic to promote universal health care, the proposition team might argue that access to medical care is important and might choose not to discuss the cost. On the other hand, the rising cost of health services might be an important issue for the opposition, who could introduce the issue early in the debate using the following POI.

> Health care costs are increasing at 2–4 times the rate of inflation. The costs are already too high. Japan, Spain, Ireland, Italy, the United Kingdom, Greece, and Canada are already cutting back on health care and other services—environmental protection, nutrition, and housing—because of increased health care costs.

You can also use POIs to misdirect your opponent so that he thinks your team will make one kind of argument while you intend to make a very different one. For example, on the topic, "States should pay minimum wage for convict labor," the opposition might use the following POI: Convicts simply do not have the skills or training to perform skilled work." The POI is a misdirection. The debater making the POI wants the speaker to disagree with her claim. She wants the speaker to say: "Convicts have significant job skills. Not only that, our case supports job training for them. They will be able to do serious work."

The opposition wants to argue that convicts will take away jobs from other workers. The POI is used to get the speaker to admit that convicts might be effective workers. If the convicts are effective, they will compete with other workers. The information from the POI helps make the argument for the opposition team.

- **Attack Arguments.** You can use POIs to prove that your opponent's arguments don't make sense, are contradicted by other arguments, have no factual support, or are denied by better historical and current examples. The opposition, in particular, should use POIs for this purpose because it has fewer stands on the floor than the proposition. A stand on the floor is an opportunity to present new information or to give an immediate reply to an opponent's position. While the proposition has three stands on the floor, the opposition has only two because the second opposition speech and the opposition rebuttal are back-to-back. Consequently, the opposition rebuttalist cannot immediately reply to the proposition's arguments nor can she offer new arguments since they are not permitted in rebuttal speeches.

To get a third stand on the floor, the opposition needs to use POIs to force the opening proposition speaker to defend her case while she is presenting it. These POIs are generally no different than arguments that the opening opposition speaker might present, but introducing them as POIs during the first proposition speech provides a strategic advantage. After listening to the proposition's replies, the opposition can make adjustments to its planned arguments, introducing stronger positions in the opening opposition speech.

For example, on the topic, "The United States should increase sentences for drug possession," an opposition speaker might begin his side's attack during the proposition team's opening speech:

> The proposition claimed that increased prosecution and sentencing of drug offenses will reduce drug use. That is not the case—it has never been true. Every time the government increases the penalties for drug possession, the price of drugs increases and criminals commit more crime to get money to pay for drugs. Drug crime increases. That is the reason that we oppose more prosecution and longer sentences for the crime of drug possession.

SUGGESTED EXERCISES

1. Practicing Heckles and Counter-heckles

Ask a volunteer to deliver a short speech (3–4 minutes). The other members of the group are to practice heckling while the speaker practices counter-heckles.

2. Practicing POIs

Ask a volunteer to deliver a short speech (3–4 minutes). All other members of the group are to attempt at least one POI. The speaker should accept 1–3 POIs and reject the others by using gestures.

3. Practicing POIs in "Real Time"

Organizing POIs during a debate is not easy because the pace is swift and you have other things to do (prepare a speech, listen to and help teammates, record notes, etc.). To help you learn to identify opportunities for POIs and organize ideas into POIs quickly, listen to a radio or TV news commentary or political speech, then practice organizing and attempting POIs.

CHAPTER 7:

TAKING NOTES

Because debates are complicated, note taking is a skill vital to success. Many debates are won or lost based entirely on note taking. Without good notes, you will not be able to structure the contents of your speech or answer your opponent's arguments and extend those of our teammates.

You have probably taken notes for your school classes—jotting down key phrases and concepts—but these types of notes do not have the sufficient rigor for debaters, who must rapidly and accurately track the progress of the arguments made and note the evidence offered by both teams. Consequently, in PDP, debaters use a special method of note taking, known as "flowing," that relies heavily on symbols and abbreviations to record information quickly. Flowing promotes direct clash because it enables you to track the progression of arguments, spot holes in your opponent's strategy, and ensure that you respond to all of the necessary arguments.

Debaters—and judges—record their notes on a flowsheet, a piece of paper, turned horizontally and divided into five columns. Once complete, the flowsheet becomes a transcript, a history of the debate.

1st Prop	1st Opp	2nd Prop	2nd Opp/OR	PR

Columns are labeled by title of speaker and organized in speech order. The first column is labeled "1st Prop" for the first speaker on the proposition team; the second column is "1st Opp" for the opening speaker for the opposition team, and so on. The opposition block is labeled "2nd Opp/OR," for the second speaker for the opposition team and the opposition rebuttalist speaker. The example below, on the topic "Schools should require uniforms for students," illustrates how a flowsheet works.

Partial Sample Flowsheet

1st Prop	1st Opp	2nd Prop.	2nd Opp/OR	PR
Schools should require uniforms for students	Mandated uniforms are a denial of free choice— it teaches students a poor lesson about fundamental rights	There are all kinds of restrictions on student behavior. They can express themselves in other ways.		
1. Clothing cost is high. Fashion industry promotes new choices each year—it is expensive to buy entirely new wardrobes.	School uniforms are expensive and not worn elsewhere so they add to a clothing budget.	School clothing choice is not that important. Uniforms are less expensive than trendy fashions. Avoids embarrassment of not having new clothes for school.		

2. Keeps focus on school, not fashion and pop culture. *(circled)* →	Cannot keep those out of discussion and distraction at school.			
3. No violence from gang clothing. *(circled)* →	There are dress codes at school that avoid these problems. Uniforms do not affect gangs. Students join if they want.			

The proposition team has offered three primary arguments in the opening proposition speech:

1. Private clothing is too expensive.

2. Clothing is a distraction from school.

3. Gang clothing leads to violence.

In the first column, listeners jot down these assertions, as well as any supporting reason, evidence, and expressions of significance.

The first opposition speaker then offers her objections to the case. This would include direct refutation (disagreement with the matter in the case) and indirect refutation (new relevant material drawn from the opposition's perspective on the topic). Listeners record this information in the first opposition speaker column. If the new material is substantial, they may use another flowsheet page and, beginning with the first opposition column, record the new arguments from the opposition speaker.

The notes are jotted down so that the arguments correspond to the issues being addressed. For example, the first opposition's response to the issue of clothing cost is recorded next to that argument from the first proposition. As the debate develops, all arguments about clothing cost will be recorded parallel to the first proposition's argument. As listeners review their notes, they can easily follow the development of an argument over the duration of the debate. This helps a debater to know what might be required for her speech and the judge to understand which team might be ahead on an issue.

Notice the circles and arrows that connect arguments. These enable the notetaker to easily tell which ideas go together and if a point has been conceded or ignored. The flowsheet allows a debater to readily track the progress of ideas, refer back to earlier ideas, and make sure she covers all relevant points.

When you flow, follow a few basic principles:

- **Abbreviate whenever possible.** Because debates proceed rapidly, with remarkable density of information and argument, you can't write each word that is said. You will have to be selective about what you write and abbreviate when you do. Try using standard abbreviations such as "Ø" for "Not," or "$" for money. Use abbreviations that make sense to you, but remember that your coach may collect your flowsheets and your partners may ask to look at them, so they have to be intelligible to them as well.

- **Put ideas next to the ones they go with.** When an argument is refuted, write the answer next to it, even if it the speaker is not following the same order as the previous speech. Keeping track of arguments horizontally will help you to see how they are answered (or not).

- **Write legibly**. Because your partner may need to refer to your notes from time to time during the debate, write legibly. Some debaters find that they cannot read their own handwriting. If this happens to you, practice will often help.

- **Space out**. Leave plenty of vertical space between individual arguments. Space ensures that your flow will not become cramped and illegible later in the debate.

- **Use symbolic notation to track argument development**. To keep track of the progression of an argument, use arrows and circles. If you make an argument that is subsequently refuted, cross it out. Star arguments that have been dropped or gone unanswered so that you will be able to point out that the other side has effectively agreed with your ideas.

- **Don't stop writing if you get lost**. Sometimes, debaters get confused about what their opponent is saying or what part of the debate he is addressing. Just keep taking notes—you might miss some critical argument or example. You shouldn't lose debates because your opponent is disorganized.

- **Practice**. You only learn to flow well if you practice.

You should flow the entire debate. Even after your speech is over, keep track of what is being said so you can help your teammates answer opponent's arguments and make sense of the judge's decision at the end of the debate. Flowsheets also serve a long-term purpose. Your partner will want a record of her speech so she can improve her presentation, and the team will want notes of your opponent's best arguments and tactics so they can utilize them in future debates.

SUGGESTED EXERCISES

1. Flowing Practice 1

Have a teammate make a short (3–4) minute speech while the rest of the group flows it.

2. Flowing Practice 2

Practice flowing a television or radio news program, such as *Face the Nation,* with guests who have various viewpoints on an issue. Work to record as much of the discussion as possible by developing a series of issue-specific abbreviations. Radio is often better practice than television because it offers a steady stream of verbal information, much like a debate. Television often has long pauses for striking visual images.

CHAPTER 8:
PREPARATION

No debater can hope to win a debate without adequate preparation. Preparation begins long before the day of the tournament as you keep abreast of current affairs and ethical issues for possible impromptu topics and conduct in-depth research for pre-announced topics. And it continues through the formal preparation time that precedes the debate, when you organize your notes, share ideas, and develop arguments.

Research

Effective debating requires the ability to do good research. You may be an eloquent speaker, but without thoroughly understanding the issue and offering good evidence to support your claims and reasoning, you will convince few that your points are correct or even valid. Many of topics in PDP debates can be technical or complex—requiring careful research to understand, analyze, and argue core proposition and opposition positions.

INITIAL STEPS

When you receive the debate topic, begin your research by talking with the people around you—those who might have some knowledge of the topic and can give you an idea of the types of arguments you might hear on both sides of the debate. Begin at your school. Administrators may have information on the issues associated with school reform and discipline (e.g., curriculum reform, school uniforms, or school investigation of online bullying). Your teachers have substantial knowledge in their fields. A biology teacher might help you if the topic is a ban on dissection in the classroom. Social studies and history teachers may be excellent sources of information on constitutional law topics such as term limits or lowering the voting age. Your school librarians can help you focus your research and assist you with key-word searches.

You might also discuss topic issues with your family or members of the community who are knowledgeable about the issue. Because many legal, social, and political activist organizations, such as Amnesty International, Greenpeace, the Democratic and Republican parties, and the ACLU are involved in public policy debates, their staffs and volunteers might be able outline the arguments on both sides of an issue. These kinds of sources are a valuable and often overlooked resource in researching and preparing arguments.

Usually, consulting school personnel, family members, and community organizations is not enough, however. At some point, you will have to find other sources of information.

STARTING WITH BLANK PAPER: SETTING A RESEARCH AGENDA

Too many debaters make the mistake of beginning their research by inserting a key phrase from their topic (perhaps the entire topic) into an online search engine. The result is predictable. The search engine takes the debater to a debate site that lists positions for and against the topic. This seems to offer satisfactory information but, in reality, does not for several reasons:

- The research results are usually obvious arguments, easily anticipated by any thoughtful debater. The information substitutes for the critical thinking you need to develop and use as you prepare for debate.

- The positions are often incomplete arguments.

- The entries rarely include source information or reference lists for further research.

- The site is available to your opponents. With both teams using the material, the results simply produce the "X, –X" and "X Y" problems.

- When using such sites, you bypass the superior resources that provide the background knowledge, methodologies, cause-effect relationships, and decision-making models that allow you to sustain arguments throughout a series of challenges from your opponents.

Rather than beginning your research on a search engine screen, start with a blank sheet of paper, blank spreadsheet, or new Word file. First brainstorm your answers to the following issue-analysis questions to help you analyze the topic and plan your research.

- What do I already know about this issue?

- What do I *not* know about this issue?

- Who is affected by this issue?

- How are they affected by this issue?

- Why is this issue important?

Issue Analysis Questions

What do I already know about this issue?

What do I *not* know about this issue?

Who is affected by this issue?

How are they affected by this issue?

Why is this issue important?

Answering these questions will encourage you to practice critical thinking, creative idea development, and interdisciplinary connections (using analogies to historical examples and issues in other subjects and fields). The process will also produce more questions. For example, using the issue-analysis questions to examine the topic "The United States should not provide foreign aid to nondemocratic countries," a debater might come up with the following questions:

- What is foreign aid? Does it include economic, military, and/or humanitarian assistance?

- What do I know about U.S. foreign aid? How is foreign aid connected to U.S. foreign policy? Is U.S. aid different now than 25, 50, or 75 years ago? How so?

- Does the United States give aid to nondemocratic countries? Which ones? What kind of aid? Does that aid depend on whether the country is allied with or hostile to the United States?

- What are the benefits and negative results of giving aid to nondemocratic countries?

As you analyze the issue, you will discover what you know and do not know, what matters and does not matter about the topic. Your answers serve as a foundation for further research, brainstorming sessions with teammates, and argument development.

NOTES AND NOTEBOOKS

Effective researchers keep notes of key words, argument ideas, and future research prospects in a research notebook. Notes for an individual article with promising material should include:

- bibliographical information (title of the periodical and the article, publication date).

- list of authors and expertise.

- general content of the argument, including methodology, reasoning, evidence, and significance.

- any limitations in the research.

Keeping careful notes will help you organize future research to address any research gaps. Research notes should be included in a searchable database or organized by topic.

SUGGESTED EXERCISE

Analyzing a Topic

Complete an Issue Analysis Form (see Appendix 1) for each of the following topics.

- Foreign aid does more harm than good.

- The United States should have compulsory voting.

- Professional sports should legalize performance-enhancing drugs.

- College education should be free.

Compare your form with those of your classmates. Work with two other students to research the topic and find answers to your questions. Then present your answers to the entire class.

Resources

Debaters use a wide variety of resources when preparing for a debate—TV, newspapers, magazines, journals, and Internet sources to name a few. Each has strengths and weaknesses because each is designed to serve a different purpose. For example, online news services emphasize immediacy, while books focus on analysis. Thus, each will play a different role in your research strategy.

CURRENT INFORMATION: TELEVISION AND NEWSPAPERS

PDP debate topics are taken directly from or closely connected to current events and major ethical controversies. Consequently, to debate effectively, you need to become more aware of the world around you by watching TV news and reading newspapers daily (either in print or online).

When watching the news and reading newspapers, list the major issues covered, and follow them as they develop. Find answers to such questions as:

- What's the event?

- Where is it happening?

- Who is affected?

- How many people are affected?

- What is happening to those people, and why do they care?

- Why is the event happening?

- What solutions are being proposed?

- Who is proposing them?

- What effects will the solutions have?

TV news broadcasts will keep you up-to-date on breaking news, but keep in mind that TV includes other resources. Documentary films and opinion commentary all support argumentation.

Newspaper coverage is more comprehensive and in-depth than television news shows because newspapers have more space and are not confined to a limited time slot. Consequently, they are good sources not only for international coverage but for state and local news as well. Major newspapers that cover international, national, and local news include:

- *The Los Angeles Times*
- *The New York Times*
- *The Wall Street Journal*
- *The Washington Post*

Include at least one foreign paper in your reading. In addition to providing international news coverage, these papers also have a different perspective on U.S. stories.

The Internet has made it relatively easy to access hundreds of national and international papers and news articles. The headlines of most major daily newspapers are available online for no charge, although you are often required to establish an account. Online news services such as AP (Associated Press) report hard news; aggregators such as The Huffington Post will collect information from many news sites, thus possibly simplifying your research.

You don't have to read all sections of a newspaper or read an entire article to gather background information on your topic. The news and business sections, as well as the editorial/opinion pages, usually will be sufficient. News and business sections will cover major social, political, and economic events. The editorial and opinion pages are comments on current controversies; they are almost like debate cases and arguments.

Newspapers cover many of the stories you see on the television news. Make sure you read the articles about these so that you can compare the information presented. How is the coverage of the issue different? Did the newspaper interview different people? Do those people seem more credible, or less? How so?

MORE IN DEPTH: PERIODICALS

Periodicals (so called because they are published at regular intervals) are valuable resources for debaters. Periodicals include popular magazines written for a general audience (e.g., *Time, National Review, Scientific American*), trade magazines produced about a specific field (e.g., *Advertising Age, Food Engineering, Oil and Gas Journal*), and peer-reviewed journals that have panels of experts who review articles and make publication suggestions to the editorial board (e.g., *African Journal of Legal Studies, Economic Perspectives, Foreign Policy*). Because periodicals do not face the daily deadlines newspapers do, they can watch an issue develop and provide thoughtful, well-researched reporting and analysis—just the thing for aspiring debaters. Therefore, magazines can often give you a better perspective on an issue. One downside of magazines is that their information can be dated because they are published less frequently.

Online proprietary services such as EBSCO and INFOTRAC can help you access periodicals as well as newspapers, reports, almanacs, dictionaries, encyclopedias, public opinion polls, government information, and the full text of books. Many school and public libraries have access to them and some allow you to access these from your home computer.

If you need to find an article in a library's physical periodical collection, consult the library's catalog for the periodical name, volume, and issue number. Then go to the shelves, where the periodicals are organized alphabetically and in volume order. Once you have located the volume, you should easily find the issue you need.

WHAT'S ON THE SHELF? USING BOOKS FOR RESEARCH

Perhaps the most obvious, and valuable, place to do research is in books. Books are likely to examine a subject in depth, with substantially more examples and research than newspapers and periodicals. Using books does have a disadvantage, however. Because preparing a book for publication takes time—the book must be edited, printed, and distributed—information may not be current. So, if you are researching a current events topic, you will have to update the material you found in books with information from newspapers and periodicals.

You don't have to read an entire book to determine if it is useful; you can gather the information you need in just a few steps. First, review the table of contents and look through the subject heads in the index to see if the book might be worthwhile. If you think it is, read the conclusion. This will give you a sense of the strength of the author's arguments and evidence, the breadth and depth of her research, and the overall relevance of the book. If the conclusion seems promising, read the opening and closing paragraphs of those chapters that look useful. Read the entire chapter only if these paragraphs look helpful.

THE INTERNET

The Internet is a vital resource for debaters because it provides easy access to a wide variety of information—government statistics, NGO reports, opinion polls, breaking news, commentary pages, blogs, and more. This advantage is also one of its biggest drawbacks. The web simply contains too much information, and often you can't tell what is accurate or best. After all, anyone can publish anything on the web, and most websites do not have editors who check facts.

Before you tackle your web research, develop a strategy. First, take a few minutes to think about what you want to get out of the search. For example, if your topic is school uniforms, you might want to research arguments and evidence for and against wearing them. Then list the key words and phrases you will use in your research (remember to put phrases in quotes). When you find a potentially useful site, bookmark it so you can return to it easily.

Critically evaluate any websites you use. Be aware of the purpose of the site. Some may have a strong bias. For example, a think tank might have a political agenda. Before using the site, ask yourself the following questions:

- Who is responsible for the information?

- Does the author have a reason to distort or change the information?

- Does the author (a person or an organization) have a membership in another organization that might influence the information?

- Is the author trying to persuade you to adopt her beliefs?

One final tip for Internet research: don't stop researching once you have found one or two promising sites. Consult a wide variety of sites to ensure that your information is fair and balanced.

Creating an Argument Agenda from Research

When you begin researching an issue, first gather background information on the subject, even if you think you know a lot about it. Reading a general article or two will help you get a better perspective on the issue and anticipate what others might say in a debate on the subject.

As you research, keep track of potential arguments for both sides of an issue. Dividing a sheet of paper, Word page, or spreadsheet into two columns—one for the proposition side and one for the opposition side—is helpful. As you continue your research, you will identify which arguments are stronger and weaker. Some issues will have more direct and powerful reasoning, more recent and clearly detailed evidence, more profound significance (consequences in individual cases and for larger groups). Other arguments will be less potent or will have lost relevance.

Adjust your research as you compile and evaluate arguments. Focus on researching and developing promising arguments; devote less time to or abandon less helpful issues; begin to anticipate, identify, research, and prepare to address opponents' potential arguments.

Finally, complete an A-R-E-S-R chart (see Chapter 10 for detailed discussion) for each likely position on both sides of the motion. This chart lists the assertion, reasoning, and evidence for each argument as well as its significance and result. Use a separate page for each argument so your team can organize them as they wish when preparing for the debate. Completing a chart for each potential argument will help you identify incomplete positions and resolve research gaps.

A-R-E-S-R Chart

POTENTIAL ARGUMENT:_____

A: Assertion:_____

R: Reasoning:_____

E: Evidence:_____

S: Significance:_____

R: Result:_____

SUGGESTED EXERCISES

1. Key Word Search

Use the *Library of Congress Subject Headings Guide* and the Internet to find key words for the term *International Criminal Court*. Practice using the key word list to begin examining the topic.

2. Library Scavenger Hunt

Use a library or the Internet to find the following:

- A legal dictionary.

- The complete text of the First Amendment to the U.S. Constitution.

- Two political quotations describing the value of democracy for human rights promotion.

- The number of people unemployed in the United States.

- The number of rebel groups fighting the Syrian government.

- The number of undocumented immigrants living in the United States.

- An argument in favor of asteroid mining in space.

- The rank of the United States on an index of infant mortality.

- The number of suicides and accidents attributable to guns.

- An important news event on March 3, 2005.

- The members of the Arab League.

- An argument in favor of government incentives for renewable energy technology.

Preparation Time

At a tournament, participants initially gather in a large central location—auditorium, media center, gymnasium, cafeteria—to view the location and pairings of debates. This information is presented a few minutes before the first debate is to begin either on paper posted in locations around the meeting space or projected on a large screen. The pairings are the matched debates, typically organized and generated using tournament tabulation software. The presentation is in four columns listing: room numbers, proposition teams, opposition teams, and judges. Read each line from left to right. For example:

Room	Proposition	Opposition	Judge
KRV 109	Sage Mount LKT	Webster GHR	Holter
KRV 161	Frontier RBN	Fairport KCP	Mackinaw
BC 36	Reardon BSK	Webster LOT	Holstege
BC 22	Cathedral ASD	La Salle LBD	Short

Teams are usually listed by the initials of the members; last names are not necessarily in alphabetical order.

When the pairing sheets are made available, the tournament director calls coaches forward to receive colored paper for their team. A different colored paper is used for each debate; the tournament director will announce that an upcoming debate is a "blue debate" or "yellow debate," letting participants know what color paper they must use. The topic is then announced and, if the motion was pre-announced, the debaters have 20 minutes to prepare. For high school PDP impromptu debates, debaters have 30 minutes preparation time. Debaters *must* be in the listed room and ready to begin when preparation time ends. There is no grace period at the conclusion of preparation time.

The PDP format sets out the rules for preparation time. These include:

- Students must organize materials for their debates during preparation time.

- Debaters may use materials they prepared in advance of the tournament but they cannot electronically access information during this time.

- Only materials prepared during preparation time may be used in the debate.

- All notes for the debate, including those the debaters prepared beforehand, must be recorded on the announced colored paper. Students who have to use electronic materials because of disabilities, may use them only to accomplish what they might otherwise do with pen and paper. For example, a debater who is permitted to use a laptop computer for note taking before and during debates may not use it to access the Internet.

- Only the students participating in the debate may transcribe notes. Coaches, parents, school volunteers, and other students may not write on colored paper to assist preparation.

- Coaching is permitted during preparation time.

- Once a debate is under way, debaters are not permitted to review any materials that have not been prepared during preparation time.

A violation of the preparation time rules is quite serious and may mean a forfeit and loss of a debate.

Debaters may prepare in the tournament's central meeting place or another convenient spot. The proposition team is entitled to prepare in the classroom where the debate is to be held but, at most sites, students cannot enter a classroom without the assigned judge. The judge might authorize entry, however.

Preparation time is a vital part of the debate, so you and your coaches should prepare strategies for efficient use and practice them before any tournament. Each team will develop its own approach, but here are some recommendations:

- **Prepare separately.** If your school has sent multiple teams to a tournament and the teams are on different sides of the topic, the proposition and opposition teams should prepare separately so they can concentrate exclusively on their side.

- **Be aware of time.** Each team should have an inexpensive digital timer to keep track of elapsed time during preparation. A second timer is valuable to track individual assignments during prep time.

- **Assign tasks.** Assign each team member a specific task. For example, one team member might prepare the opening speech; another might anticipate and prepare replies to arguments from the opponents; a third might assist argument development by identifying evidence and significance for her partner's ideas.

- **Prepare checklists.** Develop checklists (e.g., to ensure you develop complete arguments) to help jog your memory and produce more comprehensive and convincing ideas.

- **Brief arguments.** Do not write out a full speech. Doing so limits your ability to reply to issues from the other side—in other words, to debate. Prepare each argument and reply to an argument on separate sheets of paper, briefing, or outlining, each. Add a title for easy reference. When the debate is under way, you can quickly organize the sheets in the order you want to present the information.

- **Give the opening speaker practice time.** If possible, a team's second and third speakers should give enough support to the first speaker so that she can practice her speech aloud. She may not be able to practice the entire speech, but it will be more organized and persuasive if she has time to practice the initial 3–4 minutes of the presentation.

- **Prepare introductions and conclusions.** Spend time preparing speech introductions and conclusions. An effective attention getter and dramatic conclusion can give a debater an edge.

- **Prepare as much material as possible prior to the debate.** Although preparation time may seem hectic, it is usually calmer than the actual debate, when speakers will be listening to opponents, taking notes, and paying attention to time and the nonverbal signals from the judge. Include developing POIs and heckles during preparation—asking highly effective POIs and crafting argumentative heckles during the debate is very difficult.

SUGGESTED EXERCISES

1. Reduced Preparation Sessions

Practice preparation by reducing the time you have (15 minutes for pre-announced topics and 20 minutes for impromptu motions) so that the tournament preparation period will seem generous.

2. Using Impromptu Topics

Because impromptu topics are not announced prior to a competition, they are more challenging to prepare for. Formulate a topic based on a headline from the front page of a newspaper. Then practice preparing for that debate.

STRATEGY AND TACTICS

CHAPTER 9:

TOPICS AND CASE CONSTRUCTION

A topic, also known as a motion, is a statement used to start a debate. Interpreted by the proposition team, it directs the discussion.

Debates in high school PDP events include both pre-announced and impromptu topics. A pre-announced topic is one that can be prepared prior to the debate. Participants have several weeks to think about the topic, research arguments, and carefully organize their notes. Students know the topic in advance of a tournament but do not know on which side they will be arguing until a few minutes before the debate begins. Consequently, they must research both sides of the motion.

How far in advance a topic is announced depends on the type of event. Because students might have considerable knowledge of a subject related to the curriculum, a classroom debate topic might be announced several days before the debate. To ensure enough time to organize and publicize a public event, a debate for a school assembly, community group, or broadcast audience might be announced two or three months in advance. For a PDP competition, debate topics are announced approximately three to four weeks before the tournament. Topics are selected to provide a range of personal, education, social, political, economic, and cultural issues.

An impromptu topic is announced just 30 minutes before a debate begins. Once the topic is announced, debaters draw on their own knowledge to plan their arguments. Impromptu topics for high school PDP events are drawn from current events and ethical controversies.

HSPDP Pre-Announced Topics

The United States should substantially increase gas taxes.

The First Amendment should not protect hate speech.

Websites should pay consumers for data mining.

Close Guantanamo.

The U.S. should eliminate the mortgage interest tax deduction.

The United States should have a national identification card.

Eliminate super-majority legislative voting.

The United States should block jihadi websites.

The U.S. should establish term limits for Article III federal judges.

In cases of kidnapping or piracy, governments should pay ransom.

HSPDP Impromptu Topics

It is unethical to eat meat.

High school attendance should be voluntary.

NATO should withdraw from Afghanistan.

Schools should punish students for cyber-bullying.

Public financing of elections is preferable to current campaign financing arrangements.

All tax increases should require voter approval.

"Stand Your Ground" laws do more good than harm.

Schools should not have competitive sports.

President Barack Obama should return his Nobel Peace Prize.

Abolish the UN Security Council veto.

PDP Public Debate and Classroom Topics

The United States should pay reparations for slavery.

Financial bailouts do more good than harm.

The United States should adopt English as the official national language.

Torture is justified to protect national security.

The U.S. should have a military draft.

Andrew Jackson should be removed from the $20 bill.

Standardized testing does more good than harm.

The atomic bombing of Hiroshima was justified.

The North should have let the South secede.

Schools should ban animal dissection.

Types of Topics

Topics are often categorized by their wording. Some popular categories are:

- **Policy topics.** A policy topic calls for a particular course of action. When debating these topics, the proposition team will identify an existing problem and propose a hypothetical solution. Examples of policy topics include:

> Schools should be year-round.

> Professional sports should permit the use of performance-enhancing drugs.

- **Fact topics.** A fact topic requires the proposition to prove that a particular condition (a "fact") is more likely to be true than false. For example:

> The United States is in a recession.

> Undocumented immigrants have a negative economic impact in California.

Debating about facts is important because your decision about whether a statement is true or false limits your later choices and actions. For example, in 2003, whether you believed the statement "Iraq possesses weapons of mass destruction" mattered a great deal. Those who agreed with the statement were more likely to favor America's military intervention in Iraq than those who did not.

- **Value topics.** A value topic questions a particular ideal or a set of judgments about the world or may require debaters to compare values. Examples of value motions include:

> Civil disobedience is morally justified.

> A journalist's right to shield confidential sources is more important than the government's right to gather evidence.

- **Historical topics.** A historical topic asks debaters to examine the past, using eyewitness accounts, written documents, the results of forensic investigations, and other materials and insights. These topics allow students to analyze or offer a better explanation for historical events and characters. They may be fact, value or policy topics. Examples of historical topics include:

> The British Empire did more good than harm to India.

Political parties are a threat to American democracy.

Categories are not rigid and topics may fall into more than one category. Facts are used in all debates. Values and the costs and benefits of a policy may be discussed in any debate. The categorization of topics does not limit the arguments you can choose. These categories are only useful to begin thinking about strategies to prove the motion.

Interpreting the Topic

Important to remember: words may have many meanings. For example, *word* can mean an utterance, remark, a unit of language, a promise or sworn intention, news, an angry or quarreling speech, or a short conversation. Consequently, a motion may have several meanings depending on how the words it is expressed in are defined.

In a debate, the proposition team interprets the topic. The first proposition speaker defines key terms and explains what the topic means for the debate at hand. In short, the proposition establishes the decision-making framework for the debate.

The proposition narrows the motion for two reasons. First, the team simply does not have enough time in a 6-minute speech to make a case in support of all variations of the topic. For example, if the proposition were debating "Television is a bad influence," they could not create a case that considered all possible private and public television programming—news and opinion, entertainment, cultural programming, advertising, films, foreign language and American Sign Language broadcasts, religious and education programs—in all countries for the past 60 years. Obviously, the time constraints make such broad-ranging presentation impossible.

Second, the proposition must present a single and coherent case. Again, this is impossible if they have to address all possible arguments on the topic. On the topic "The U.S. should substantially reduce greenhouse gas emissions," many arguments suggest that market incentives would be the best way to reduce greenhouse gas emissions—but many also argue in support of government regulations as a solution to the problem. The proposition team cannot be expected to create a case from contradictory arguments about market incentives and government policies.

The proposition team is expected to interpret the motion in a reasonable manner. They must offer a definition that is predictable and clearly linked to the motion. For example, if the topic is "The United States should abolish the death penalty," they cannot define "death penalty" as referring to the estate tax (the tax, a "penalty," on an individual's assets [the estate] after death) or NCAA suspension of college athletic scholarships (punishment for violation of athletic program rules) both of which are known as "death penalty." The definition must also be debatable. It must permit substantive arguments on both sides of the issue, and it cannot force the opposition to defend the indefensible—for example, asking the opposition to defend murder.

The opposition cannot challenge a definition simply because they have not anticipated the proposition's case or because they would prefer to debate an easier one. Unless a definition is off topic, they must debate the motion as the proposition defines it. Can the opposition never challenge a definition? Certainly they can. But the opposition cannot simply assert that a definition is unreasonable or undebatable or assume that the judge will intervene. They must offer arguments pointing out the specific statements in the opening proposition speech that make the definition so unreasonable or undebatable that the debate should not have been held.

Challenging a definition is rarely successful because the opening proposition speech almost always contains arguments in support of the motion. Sometimes these arguments are explicit; in other cases, they are implied. That these arguments are not explicitly offered does not mean that they are not present in the speech. Instead of challenging the definition, the opposition team should argue that the proposition's case fails to meet the proposition's own interpretation of the motion.

1. Narrowing topics

Choose a topic from the list in Appendix 2 and give yourself 5 minutes to narrow the motion. You must explain:

- Why is it a reasonable interpretation?

- How is the interpretation convincing to a judge?

2. Defining topics

Working with a partner or in a small group, choose a topic from Appendix 2. Then take 5 minutes to prepare as many different definitions as you can.

Introduction to Case Construction

If you are debating the proposition, you will present a case that contains a number of conceptual arguments in support of the motion. The term *case* comes to us from the law; prosecutors make a case against the defendant by presenting evidence to prove his guilt. When you make a case for the topic, you present evidence to prove the motion. But just as a prosecutor would not present all the evidence available in random order, you would not present every argument possible on the motion. You would select your strongest arguments and present them in the most persuasive way to create a logical proof of the topic.

If the proposition team can prove the case for the motion—that the motion is more likely to be true than false—it will likely win the debate. So, they must invest time and care when planning and constructing their case. The proposition team may seem to have the advantage in the debate because they interpret the motion and have the last speech in the debate; the opposition, however, has 11 minutes of back-to-back speeches (the opposition block) giving them an equally significant advantage. Consequently, the proposition team must develop their case wisely.

CASE CHOICE

Teams have many options when deciding how to prove the topic. Some students are drawn to unusual or very narrow interpretations of motions, thinking that the element of surprise will give them the win. Unfortunately, this is not so. Effective opposition teams learn to brainstorm and prepare for unusual cases—even if they are caught off guard, they have the skills to take their existing arguments and apply them in new situations. Also, judges have expectations for the motion, thus failing to meet them is not a sound way to begin the debate. Judges may also give more credit to the arguments of an opposition team who tries to debate a more challenging definition. The proposition team actually has an advantage presenting a predictable case: they can more easily anticipate opposition arguments and plan a strategy for each of their speeches. Consequently, choosing more obvious interpretations is more likely to be a winning strategy.

Preparation is the key to the proposition winning debates. As you research your topic, keep notes on the different cases you might use. This strategy not only helps you prepare your case but will also help you better anticipate opposition arguments. Knowing what the strongest opposition arguments are will help you counter them and prepare you should you draw the opposition position in the debate.

Once you have a range of case ideas, don't immediately choose your approach based on your instant favorite. Think strategically. Consider the strongest arguments the opposition can offer and then choose a case based on your ability to respond to or capture these. For example, if you will be debating the topic "Students should be drug-tested for after-school activities," your research has shown you that that one of the major arguments for the opposition is that students have a right to privacy. You need to think about how you will respond to this argument *before* you choose how to make your case. You might say that privacy is actually an advantage of mandatory drug testing because it will reduce more invasive practices like locker searches and increased police presence on school campuses. Whether you present this argument in the first speech or wait to present it as a response is up to you; your primary consideration is to have thought about how you will respond and selected the arguments to build your case accordingly.

Case selection and organization can differ slightly depending on whether you are debating a policy, fact, or value motion.

Proving Policy Topics

To prove a policy topic, you must make a persuasive case for a course of action. To do so your case must:

- **Establish a need for change.** First show why there is a need for change or a harm that exists in the present state of affairs (sometimes called the "status quo"). Let's say the topic is "Schools should ban junk food." You might argue that schools provide a wide variety of junk food and demonstrate why access to junk food is bad.

- **Present a solution.** Offer a plan, your proposed solution to the problem. The plan should have specific details and include three elements:

  - *Agent.* Identify the individual, institution, or organization with the authority to carry out your plan. For example, using the topic, "Arm the Syrian rebels," the proposition team might argue that the Arab League should be the agent responsible for providing arms. Be specific. If the federal government is to implement your plan, indicate which branch or agency will do it.

  - *Mandate or directive.* Explain what action you want taken. This action could be simple, for example, establishing a set of modest guidelines, or more complex if the topic and case suggest technical or broad reforms, such as instituting a market-based pollution emission trading system or setting out the conditions for using force and exiting from a humanitarian military intervention. The plan might also include assessment—formal directives that establish that policy reforms will be audited and evaluated to maximize beneficial outcomes—and sunset provisions that determine when the action will end or be subject to review and reapproval.

- *Enforcement.* Set out how the policy will be implemented and what might happen to any individual or group who resists or violates its procedure. Who will enforce your plan? Will a violation be a civil or criminal offense? If the plan requires international action, make sure you state how international law can be applied—enforcing laws across independent, sovereign national jurisdictions is difficult.

- **Show that the plan works to resolve the problems you identified.** Logically prove that your plan solves the problem. Proposing that regulating gas lawn mowers will solve global warming is not likely to work. Your plan must be technically possible (you can't use magic to solve the world's problems) and able to accomplish its goals in a relatively short time (you can't wait to the year 2313 for a solution).

SUGGESTED EXERCISE

Practicing Case Making: Propositions of Policy

Make a simple case for "Students should be required to wear uniforms." Think of a variety of plans, including the type of uniforms and different ways those requirements might be enforced. Then brainstorm the opposition's likely arguments, pick the best one, and defend your plan against it.

Proving Fact Topics

Debating propositions of fact is challenging because we usually do not think that facts are arguable. Instead, we are likely to define a fact as a true piece of information. The idea that facts are not debatable is mistaken, however. At one time, everyone agreed on these facts: the Sun revolved around the Earth and the Earth was flat.

In debate, you will not likely have to prove or disprove widely accepted scientific laws. It is more likely that you will have to debate about facts that are controversial or subject to challenge. How do you prove a scientific hypothesis? You have to test it and produce a compelling body of evidence that the hypothesis is valid. To prove a proposition of fact, you do the same.

When proving a motion of fact, use a four-step process:

1. **Determine how to prove the topic.** Define the terms of the topic so you can answer the question: Under what circumstances would this statement be valid?

2. **Brainstorm arguments for the topic.** Think of as many arguments as you can to prove the motion. Try adding "because" to the end of the topic to help you find reasons that it might be true.

3. **Organize those arguments, picking two to four to serve as major points in your speech.** Categorize the arguments you've brainstormed, putting similar arguments together. Then, pick your strongest arguments—usually those for which you have found the best evidence.

4. **Fill in your case by adding evidence to prove each point.** Using your research as well as knowledge gained from your own experience, add examples to prove each of your major points.

Let's look at how you would employ this process with the proposition "The welfare system does not work." First, you will have to define your terms so that everyone understands what it would mean to agree that the system does not work. To establish that the welfare system does not work, you will have to show that it does not perform its designated function. At this point in your analysis, you have answered the question: Under what circumstances would this statement be valid? If you can show that the welfare system does not perform its designated function, then you have proved that the proposition is true.

Now that you've analyzed *how* to prove the proposition, you would brainstorm arguments about the topic. What do you expect welfare systems to do? You expect a social safety net to keep people out of poverty. You expect that welfare will, in particular, help the most fragile elements of society—for example, children, the physically or mentally disabled, the frail elderly. Finally, you might expect that our welfare system would help the unemployed return to the workforce. You might use each expectation as a segment of your case, structuring each as a separate line of argument or independent proof of the motion. A simple preliminary outline of your case for the motion might look like this:

- Definition of terms and explanation of strategy for proving the motion.

- The welfare system does not work because it does not keep people out of poverty.

- The welfare system does not work because it does not protect the most fragile elements of society, such as children, the mentally or physically disabled, or the frail elderly.

- The welfare system does not work because it does not help unemployed people get back into the workforce.

Here, we have simply transferred the expectations we brainstormed into the form of arguments. We've taken the assertion of the topic, "The welfare system does not work," and offered three different reasons to prove that assertion. But following the A-R-E model presented in Chapter 1, these arguments are not complete. The next step of constructing this case is to add evidence for each of these lines of reasoning.

When you construct a case on a proposition of fact, you should advance at least three different lines of argument as your proof of the motion. It is important to emphasize that each of these reasons can be considered independently—you should argue that if you establish any one of these arguments, you should win the debate because you will have proved that, in this instance, the welfare system does not work. Strategically, you want to make more than one argument for the motion in the first proposition speech to maximize your options for later in the debate. Making only one argument in the first speech is foolish because you will be in a bad position if the opposition team is able to answer that argument or, worse, is able to *turn* it (make it into an argument for their side). If, during the course of the debate, you think an argument is not working, you can always narrow your position.

Once you have these parts of your case complete and you have written an outline for your argument for the motion, you should make sure that you add an introduction, a conclusion, and appropriate transitions between your major points.

SUGGESTED EXERCISES

1. Completing Propositions of Fact

Find evidence for each of the three lines of reasoning presented in the welfare system example above and integrate them into the case outline to complete the proof of the topic. In your opinion, which of the three claims is the strongest? Which is the weakest? In your research, what other arguments did you find that might support this topic? What arguments and evidence did you find that might support the opposition side? You might work with a partner or a small group to accomplish this assignment.

2. Working with Propositions of Fact

Using what you have learned, construct a case to prove the following proposition of fact: "Viruses are alive."

Proving Value Topics

A value case provides a proof for the motion by proving that a specific value is good or that the specific value is better than another value to which it is opposed. Proving that a value is good can be difficult, however. How do you explain, for example, that liberty is good or is something that we should value? How about safety? Why do we believe that safety is good? Now, what if the two are in conflict? If you think dealing with values is complicated, you are right. Issues of value have been debated for thousands of years, but we are still having significant debates about these same values.

One of the reasons we continue to debate values is because values are abstract ideas that mean different things to different people in different circumstances. For example, many people talk about "family values," but they can't agree on what that means. Do all families look the same? Do they all behave in the same way? Do they all have the same values? This diversity of perspectives guarantees that "family values" will have many definitions.

Values may also contain contradictory meanings. For example, we all experience liberty both when we are independent and when we are in dependence. We experience freedom when we are able to do what we want. You also experience freedom when someone else protects us.

Consider that nobody wants the government to control their lives, since that would restrict their freedom. However, most people want to win the lottery, even though having the government provide their income for life is a pretty serious dependence on the government. Yet we can all agree that it would be liberating to win the lottery because we would be free of the constraints of having to earn a living and could do (within the law) or buy whatever we want.

Because the meaning of values varies, do not try to prove that values are good in the abstract or in general terms. You have to look at a specific circumstance to determine whether you will endorse a particular value. For example, agreeing that you support liberty in the abstract is meaningless because that support needs context. Most people are in favor of liberty, but they would not argue that another person has the freedom to kill them. If you are in favor of freedom, but not the freedom of someone else to kill you, you have limited the definition of liberty. You are in favor of a kind of liberty that does you no harm. To make a case for a value, pick a specific scenario or policy to serve as a proof of the topic.

Many value topics compare two values and ask the proposition team to show why we should endorse one value rather than the other. Let's see how we would make a case for the topic "This House would value security over personal freedoms" using the four-step process outlined above. How would you go about proving this proposition? As you already know, you first need to interpret the topic and define your terms because the statement is too vague to be proven in the abstract. You will need to explain what you mean by security and personal freedom and answer questions such as: Personal freedom to do what? Whose security? Who provides the security?

When you brainstorm your arguments, think of examples that prove your interpretation of the proposition. To prove our sample topic, you would have to come up with specific situations in which security is more important than personal freedom. For example, most societies have legal limits on who can own a gun and on what kind of guns these people can own. This is a situation in which society has agreed that security is more important than personal freedom. It would be very dangerous, for example, to have convicted murderers wandering around with automatic weapons.

Narrowing your focus to gun control is the beginning of your case. To prove the topic, you will need to make a case for gun control. What arguments can you make for it? Those who advocate gun control argue that it would reduce violent crime because people would not be able to use guns in disputes. Gun control might also save children's lives. Every year in the United States alone, thousands of children die in gun-related accidents. Finally, you need to argue these risks to personal security are more important than the potential harm to personal freedom. All three of these arguments for gun control might become major points in your case for the topic. If you determine that these are your major points, you would add evidence to prove each.

Think of this case for the topic using the A-R-E model. The *assertion* is the topic: "This House would value security over personal freedoms." The *reasoning* can be found in your basic case statement: "Safety from guns is more important than the personal freedom to own guns." Finally, the *evidence* for the overall proof of the motion is found in your other arguments that show the costs of gun violence to be high and the potential impact of restricting ownership on personal liberties relatively low.

SUGGESTED EXERCISE

Practicing Value Topics

Using the four-step process, practice making different cases for the value topics: "This House would endorse the right to privacy" and "Free speech should be restricted."

CHAPTER 10:
SIGNIFICANCE AND RESULTS

In Chapter 1 you learned that a formal argument includes three elements: an assertion, reasoning, and evidence. But just offering complete arguments will not win you debates because you could have weak arguments: ideas that include reasoning and evidence but just do not matter to individuals and have little consequence for many people. To debate effectively, you have to add two more components to your argument structure: significance and result. Significance explains why your idea is important. But your opponent might also have significant ideas. Consequently, to win, you also need a result, an explanation of why your idea is superior to those of your opposition and that it might, in and of itself, be a proof of the motion or overwhelm the opponent's proof. Adding significance and result gives you a complete argument position structure—A(ssertion)–R(easoning)–E(vidence)–S(ignificance)–R(esult)—and makes your argument stand out from other ideas. It is a position that is a winner.

Complete Argument Position Structure

A: Assertion

R: Reasoning

E: Evidence

S: Significance

R: Result

Understanding Significance

Significance refers to both the consequences that affect a single individual (qualitative significance) and the number of people ultimately affected (quantitative significance). For example, consider the loss of privacy associated with warrantless wiretapping. How important is that loss to an individual (qualitative significance)? How many people are subject to warrantless wiretaps (quantitative significance)? If you can prove that your argument has both qualitative and quantitative significance, you will increase its authority, strength, and meaningfulness.

Do not assume that you, the judge, and the other debaters agree on what is significant for the purpose of evaluating the debate. You must explain why your argument matters. For example, just arguing that "Children should watch less television because it affects them negatively" is weak. You need to say *how* watching too much television affects them and *how many* children are affected.

Most debates are won or lost based on the explanation of significance. To prove significance—and consistently win debates—you must appeal both to the reason and the emotions of your judge. Significance can inform the judge of the importance of an issue and persuade the judge emotionally. To make significance persuasive, you must flesh it out and personalize it. You must help the judge visualize the potential consequences of the issue in a way that makes it important and meaningful. If an argument has qualitative significance, the circumstance you describe might be meaningful to the judge. She might wonder "What if that happened to me?" If not part of this larger set of individuals, she might imagine people who she knows as part of that group.

Significance adds substance to an argument and should also establish a personal and emotional connection from the argument to the imagination of the judge. For example, you *could* just say: "Our proposal is good because it brings people out of poverty." *Or*, you could use a variety of substantive and persuasive techniques to make your argument more tangible.

> Millions of people, many of them children, are malnourished in our country because of serious poverty, and few of these have any hope of making a meaningful life for themselves. Malnutrition undermines academic performance; it inhibits school success, trapping hundreds of thousands of children in a cycle of poverty. It weakens the body's immune system. The victims of food insecurity and malnutrition risk serious morbidity and mortality from common diseases—measles, mumps, influenza—because their bodies cannot reduce or eliminate the ravages of illness. Of course, hunger is painful. Chronic hunger is a great source of human suffering. Then, imagine what a tremendous help our proposal would be. Increasing welfare payments would give poor families a real chance at life and would, over time, improve the quality of life for millions and millions of individuals by protecting them from the terrible toll of hunger and malnutrition.

If you have trouble elaborating on significance, try thinking in terms of "because." Begin with a significance claim such as: "The loss of the ozone layer is bad." Then expand on it by using a series of "because" statements:

The loss of the ozone layer is bad . . . *Because* . . . More UV radiation will reach the surface of the Earth, and that's bad . . . *Because* . . . Many people will get skin cancer as a result, and that's bad . . . *Because* . . . Skin cancer is often fatal and will become more fatal as UV intensity increases.

Remember, judges like to vote for a clearly expressed and satisfactorily detailed risk or benefit. If you can convince them that your risks or benefits are more powerful and tangible, you will win more debates.

SUGGESTED EXERCISE

Explaining Significance

Explain why each of the following issues has a negative consequence and explain how many people might be affected (i.e., create qualitative and quantitative significance). If you have trouble generating explanations, use the "because" method.

- crime
- drought
- failing a class
- famine
- floods
- forest fires

- global warming
- imprisonment
- inequality
- losing the freedom of speech
- sexism
- slavery

Establishing Results: Comparing Ideas

Debate is not just about making arguments. It is also about answering those from the other side and showing why your arguments beat theirs. One way to do this is to compare arguments and, in so doing, reach the conclusion that your position is the better idea. In a debate on "The United States should lower the voting age," the proposition team might argue that lowering the voting age to 16 years will encourage more young people to participate in the electoral process. The opposition might counter that lowering the voting age is a bad idea because this age group is irresponsible and will make bad electoral decisions.

Each side would then explain the significance of their arguments. The proposition would amplify their position by arguing that if the voting age were lowered, more young people would be included in one of the key elements of citizenship, voting. If more young people voted, they could influence the outcome of elections and, consequently, future policy. Youth have a particular interest in issues such as education and the economy that require decades of public and private investment to produce results. Young voters would support candidates interested in long-term investment strategies in areas that will benefit tens of millions of people by widening opportunities for education and creating good jobs.

The opposition would answer that young people do not have the life experiences and critical thinking skills necessary to assess the strengths and weaknesses of candidates and evaluate their positions. Young people will be too easily manipulated by advertising, peer pressure, and social networking. The opposition might point out that 16-year-olds are not eligible to sign a contract, join the military, or serve on a jury. They might not have a driver's license or hold a job. They have not practiced the skills of citizenship or independent living long enough to carefully consider appropriate candidates. Consequently, youth voting might tip an election in favor of a poor candidate, one who will not make sound decisions about the future. The proposition argument presumes that the candidates young people support will make responsible decisions about education and the economy. But youth do not have the maturity or wisdom to ensure that only those candidates are elected. They do not vote in large numbers now—they are among the most apathetic and poorly informed voters. Extending the vote to even younger voters magnifies that problem. Poor candidates and elected officials will make unsound or reckless public policy decisions. They will not be satisfactory leaders on education and the economy; they will also negatively affect other public policy matters and will profoundly hurt the lives of an even greater number.

Whose argument is more substantial? Which side made the results of their position more tangible? How did they do that? Judges decide these questions by weighing the results. They use a mental scale to determine whose arguments carry greater weight and why. In this case, the judge would weigh the proposition's significance of long-term benefit to education and the economy against the opposition's significance of more uninformed voting.

The judge weighs both teams' results based on the following:

- Do the arguments support the core of the A-R-E-S-R model? Which argument has:

  - better reasoning?

  - better evidence?

  - superior significance?

- Is the result more probable? Does the position establish a clear, direct cause-and-effect relationship guaranteeing the likelihood of a positive outcome?

- Is the result more likely in the short term? Will the benefits accumulate faster and to more people over time (or will the result avert an impending disaster)?

- Is there a moral duty to act? Is the issue of such grave importance that ethically we must act immediately? Is it a simple case of right and wrong and one must take the right side?

Debaters should communicate the comparative results of arguments directly to the judge. This is referred to as "meta-debating"—debating about the debate. Do not be afraid to speak to the judge directly about the other team's arguments when comparing them. Statements like "This argument is more important than X because . . . " or "When we win this argument, we win the debate because . . . " help the judge understand the relationship among arguments.

SUGGESTED EXERCISE

Analyzing Results

Below are several pairs of competing results. Pick a pair and show why one is more important than the other. Then show how the other result is more important. Remember to include a "because" statement, and don't forget to make your arguments tangible and significant.

Privacy protection vs. national security

Economic growth vs. environmental sustainability

Free speech vs. protection of hate speech

Lifetime job security vs. judicial term limits

Civil disobedience vs. respect for the law

Private ownership of handguns vs. safety

CHAPTER 11

OPPOSITION STRATEGY

You have already learned about each team's responsibilities in a debate. The proposition tries to prove its case, which supports the motion. The opposition tries to undermine this case by challenging it directly as well as by bringing up relevant new information. The opposition arguments must overwhelm the case, proving it false in all respects or demonstrating more associated costs than benefits. Remember: the proposition is responsible only for showing that its case is more likely to be true than false (they do not have to prove that the case is true beyond a reasonable doubt or true in all circumstances). This chapter will explain how to refute a case and improve your skills when you are the opposition.

Refuting the Case

To win the debate, the opposition team must argue against the specific case the proposition presents. They cannot argue against what they hoped or imagined the case would be nor can they argue in general terms against the topic. Doing so would produce the X Y problem discussed in Chapter 5—there would be no clash. The proposition has made a case, and the opposition must expose its weaknesses and overwhelm it through direct and indirect argumentation.

The opposition speakers should account for all major arguments in the case, but they do not have to *disprove* all these ideas. In fact, as you learned in Chapter 5, they may use strategic agreement to assert that a proposition argument actually works against their case. They should consider making a challenge to the reasoning, evidence, and significance of the primary arguments in the case. And, important, the opening speaker should present new ideas—indirect refutation—that are relevant and overpowering.

The opposition needs to overwhelm the proposition team's case, but they do not do so based on the quantity of arguments they offer. Quality is more important than quantity; argument substance matters. If the proposition cannot prove its case because of just one opposition argument, the opposition side will prevail. Consequently, the opposition should challenge the key arguments that could affect the outcome of the debate.

Indirect Refutation

A successful opposition is based not only on direct refutation—challenging the reasoning and evidence supporting the specific arguments made by the opposing team—but also on indirect refutation. As you learned in Chapter 5, indirect refutation is presenting any relevant argument that is not specific to the opponent's previously stated position. If you think about it, the proposition team cannot mention everything in a relatively brief speech. It's physically impossible, no matter *how* fast they talk. In addition, the proposition team may decide to mention some issues and not to mention others to make their case as strong as it can be. In some situations, you may need to bring up issues they *did not* mention. New arguments from the opposition side can identify weaknesses, poor analysis, logical gaps, misuse of data, unintended consequences, mistaken assumptions, and other problems with the proposition case.

Let's say you are debating the topic: "It is unethical to eat meat." The proposition's case says that we have an ethical obligation to protect the rights of all creatures, and so we should agree that eating meat is unethical. You could bring up a different point: that if we agree it is unethical to eat meat (using animals as mere means), we are also agreeing that it is unethical to use animals for other purposes such as vaccine testing and to develop other medical treatments for humans. You could argue that this other purpose saves many hundreds of millions of lives, and vaccines might improve animal health in addition to that of people. The proposition did not introduce this issue in its case, but the argument may be important for deciding who wins the debate. If you brought up this issue, you would be *indirectly* refuting the case.

Organizing the Presentation Against the Case

Each speaker on the opposition team should concentrate on structuring arguments for clarity, persuasiveness, and effectiveness, but it is particularly important for the opening speaker because her speech serves as the opposition's framework for the debate. The opening speaker must make at least two major decisions: Will I begin with direct or indirect refutation? and Will I follow the organizational structure of the proposition team's case?

Usually how the speaker begins the body of her speech—direct or indirect refutation—does not matter. If the speaker is introducing new arguments, she might want to begin with indirect refutation because new points take longer to explain as no foundation has been laid for them in the debate. The speaker usually determines which approach to use based on proposition case specifics and opportunities for introducing strong arguments against their assertions.

The second question is a bit easier for most debaters. Unless a compelling reason is present to reorganize the debate, the opposition should follow the case outline. By the time the first opposition speaker rises to speak, the case has been presented and its structure is known to both teams and the judge. The judge would have to alter her note-taking if the debate is reorganized, and she might find it more difficult to follow the course of the debate.

The first opposition speaker should follow the organizational structure of the opening proposition speech even if that speech is confusing, but she should spend more time connecting ideas and explaining issues to the judge. Judges appreciate the effort that debaters make to clarify and organize a debate.

The first opposition speaker should use the general structure of the case to signpost her arguments. A signpost is language that clearly states which argument or group of arguments a speaker is addressing. Signposting is the first step of the Four-Step Method of Refutation, the "they say . . . " step. For example, the opposition speaker might say:

> In their first argument, the proposition described the scope of the housing problem. Let's begin with that description. Two things are wrong with it. First, the research is outdated. In its most recent annual review, the Department of Housing and Urban Development indicated that considerably more low-income housing was available than in the past. Second, the proposition's research concerns homelessness. But advocates for the homeless say that more available housing is not the answer to that social problem. Too many homeless are on the streets because of mental illness, lack of education, or little family and friend support. The problem needs a comprehensive public policy solution, not more housing vouchers.

The speaker might then move on to the next major issue. Of course, as we learned in Chapter 5, the speaker is not obliged to answer every argument, just account for them. The opening speaker for the opposition might get to the second argument and say, "The proposition's second position is that housing vouchers are a workable solution to the problem. I will not discuss that now but will offer a number of arguments later in my speech about what is wrong with a voucher plan." After refuting the case, the speaker would present new arguments in support of her side. These arguments should also be clearly organized so that everyone can follow and record them on a flowsheet.

Even the most inexperienced judge would have no problem following this speech. Arguments adhere to the established organizational model of the proposition case. The speaker presents information about how and why she has organized her speech in the way she has so that the judge can follow her reasoning and take careful notes. The speaker addresses her opponent's major arguments without getting bogged down in detail. She summarizes the opponent's position to briefly express it; she groups ideas together and answers them as a group when it is appropriate to do so. Finally, she clearly introduces new arguments for her side.

SUGGESTED EXERCISES

1. Practicing Refutation

Using the Four-Step Method of Refutation, refute each of the following:

All tax increases should require voter approval.

The U.S. should have a draft for military service.

Schools should not assign homework.

Voting should be mandatory.

Violence is justified against authoritarian governments.

Students should be fluent in a foreign language to graduate from high school.

Free speech should not protect hate speech.

Television is a bad influence.

The U.S. government should increase gas taxes.

Parents should not buy war toys for their children.

States should ban all cell phone use by drivers.

A lottery of qualified candidates should be used for college admission.

Lower the voting age to 16.

California should ban smoking.

2. Develop Arguments for Both Sides

Develop arguments for both sides on any of the following topics and practice arguing that the proposition argument is superior to that of the opposition. Then reverse sides and prove that the opposition positions are superior. Practice using direct and indirect refutation. Which works better and why? How does establishing significance help you compare arguments in your favor?

The United States should abolish the death penalty.

Affirmative action policies do more harm than good.

Hydrofracking does more good than harm.

U.S. Supreme Court proceedings should be televised.

Student bystanders should be punished for failing to stop bullying.

Wikipedia does more harm than good.

Advanced Opposition Arguments

DEFENSIVE AND OFFENSIVE ARGUMENTS

During a debate, participants offer two kinds of arguments: defensive and offensive. A defensive argument maintains a team's position and prevents a team from losing the debate. An offensive argument puts pressure on an opponent and provides a specific reason why an opponent has lost the debate.

While you want to play good defense against the proposition team's major points, defensive arguments will not win you the debate. Defensive arguments may help you reduce the merit of the case, but they will not prove that the proposition's case has *no* merit. If you reduce the results of the case, some merit remains. Adopting the case is still a "good," and it is likely that the "good" team will win. To win, you must use offensive arguments to show why the proposition's case is not only wrong, but also bad or dangerous. It makes the problem worse; it has more costs than benefits.

For example, if a proposition speaker argued that mandatory comprehensive vaccinations would save 2,000 lives annually, the opposition might refute it with defensive arguments by challenging the research that showed a potential for 2,000 lives saved. They might argue that, even with mandatory vaccinations, a significant minority would not participate in vaccination programs. They might also argue that governments or courts might permit religious and health exemptions for vaccinations, thus also reducing the number of people getting vaccinations. If their arguments reduced the number of lives saved by 75% but the opposition had no additional arguments, who would win the debate?

Obviously the proposition would win because they are trying to save lives. Although their position has been substantially reduced, the team's policy would still save 500 lives. They have an advantage, a benefit, and there is no cost. The proposition team is supporting a good idea. It is a smaller good than their argument at the beginning of the debate, but it is still a *good*.

Below are two examples of arguments followed by defensive and offensive responses. Notice how much stronger the offensive response is.

Example 1

Speaker: The United States should ban boxing. It is a dangerous sport and fighters risk their health.

Defense: Don't ban boxing. It is possible to use national boxing organizations to add regulations to make the sport safer. That can better protect fighters' health.

Offense: Banned boxing will go underground. Underground boxing will not have trainers, doctors, or rules. The fights will not be organized or managed with fair rules. Many more boxers will be hurt, perhaps killed, with a boxing ban.

In this example, the defensive argument acknowledges that boxing is harmful but suggests that the harm might be minimized. Will the harm be eliminated? It is hard to imagine how physical damage, particularly chronic injury from a lifetime of boxing matches, could be eliminated so that boxers would face no risks in the ring. The offensive argument recognizes that boxing is inherently dangerous but makes the point that a ban makes the problem worse.

Example 2

Speaker: The United States should have a military draft. If the public is more directly involved in military conflict, they will be less likely to support the use of the military as an instrument of foreign policy and the United States would be less likely to go to war.

Defense: The public can be educated about the costs and benefits of war. The public can persuade members of the administration and Congress to avoid risky military operations in other countries.

Offense: The U.S. military has to be prepared to go to war. The government must be able to use the military when necessary. The world is too dangerous—revolutions, terrorists, civil war, severe human rights violations, nuclear proliferation—for the United

States to wait to organize popular support for military action. The U.S. might need to intervene in countries that the public cannot find on a map. Delaying military action might increase the likelihood of attacks on U.S. citizens or facilities abroad or even attacks against the United States. This will mean the deaths of innocent people and the subsequent and extreme U.S. military reaction to an attack. The proposition team is right—they will make military action unlikely, which is dangerous in a hostile world.

Example 2 agrees with the proposition side's major argument and captures it for their side. This is an example of an offensive argument as a *turn*, an argument strategy discussed in Chapter 5.

Problem–Solution Debating

The overwhelming majority of debate topics are calls for action. They presume or identify an ongoing issue and suggest a hypothetical reform, for example: "The Supreme Court Justices should have term limits" or "The United States should negotiate with terrorists." Most proposition cases are thus logically organized in a problem–solution framework.

Usually, the opposition cannot counter the case by disproving the problem. After all, problems exist. But problems exist *because* designing workable solutions for them is difficult. Solutions have trade-offs and unanticipated consequences. For example, a solution may work for one country but not for others, or it may succeed in the short term but prove counterproductive in the long run. The proposition has a harder time finding and defending solutions than identifying problems. Consequently, focusing their refutation on the solution rather than the problem is the opposition's best strategy.

Refuting the Solution: Disadvantages, Counterplans, and Critiques

Debaters use three complementary kinds of arguments to refute solutions: disadvantages, counterplans, and critiques. All three are offensive arguments; each proves that a proposed solution (also known as a "plan," "model," or "reform") would do more harm than good. The difference among them is the perspective used to reveal the harm.

DISADVANTAGES

A disadvantage is an argument that directly analyzes the proposition's solution and reveals a cost instead of a benefit. It explains how the proposition's case, despite its good intentions, will actually exacerbate the problem. For example, if the topic of the debate was "The United States should add African lions to the endangered species list," the proposition team would identify the problem and propose a solution.

Problem: In the past century, the African lion population has plummeted from more than 200,000 to just over 30,000.

Solution: The U.S. Fish and Wildlife Service should add African lions to the endangered species list. This would make importing lions or lion pelts illegal. Government action would also highlight the plight of African lions and educate the public about the destruction of the lions' habitat and the loss of species diversity in Africa.

The opposition team would carefully analyze the proposed reform, but where the proposition found benefits, the opposition would find costs:

Adding African lions to the endangered species list will signal that few lions remain in the world. This will increase the value of lions as a commodity. Hunters, zoos, poachers, and others will want the "last of the lions." Lions and their skins will become more valuable in legal and black markets. Because the price will increase, lions will be more valuable to hunters in countries other than the United States. Poachers will also take advantage: a single lion carcass might produce enough income for a poacher for several years. Rhinos are on the critically endangered list and rhino poaching is increasing. This will be the fate of lions if the proposition proposal is adopted.

Structuring a Disadvantage

A disadvantage must have three components:

- **Link.** The link explains why adopting the proposition's plan would cause a problem or set in motion a chain of events that will lead to a problem. In presenting the link, refer to the proposition's specific language or proposed action. What did they argue or propose that causes the negative consequence? A link may have an extended chain of logical connections leading to the harm. This section of the argument is the reasoning of the argument.

- **Significance.** Once the connection is established and explained, describe the negative consequence, *the cost*, associated with the argument.

- **Result.** Finally, explain how the significance of the opposition's argument matters more than the benefits introduced by the proposition. The result explains to the judge why your team has won.

Although optional, three additional elements will help you present a more nuanced disadvantage scenario:

- **Uniqueness.** A uniqueness argument asserts that no problem exists in the status quo. The opposition might argue that without the plan there will be no problem, but with the plan there will be.

- **Brink.** The brink indicates that the disadvantage is on the verge of happening and that the proposition's reform will precipitate the harm.

- **Time Frame.** The time frame is the amount of time it takes for the onset of the problem that the disadvantage presents. If the disadvantage has a short time frame, the problems associated with the proposition plan might happen before whatever good the plan creates is achieved.

Practicing Disadvantages

Working in small groups, have half the group develop a short case on a topic of their choice; have the other half develop a disadvantage against it. Then switch sides. Clearly label link, significance, and result.

COUNTERPLANS

This type of argument has a slightly different perspective than a disadvantage. The counterplan refutes the case by taking issue with the proposition's significance arguments. But, like a disadvantage, it proves the proposition has more cost than benefit.

In presenting a counterplan, the opposition is asking the judge to weigh opportunity costs—what opportunities are lost by accepting the proposition's course of action. For example, if the proposition wants universal Medicare for U.S. citizens, they will be losing other health care options. The U.S. government could not choose to adapt another country's plan (for example, a version of the German or Canadian universal health care systems), or have states experiment with different health care options. Economists argue that every decision we make has opportunity costs.

When an opposition team offers a counterplan, they try to establish that the missed opportunity is far greater than the total benefits gained from the proposition plan. In fact, the cost is so great that the counterplan's opportunity cost, in and of itself, is a reason to reject the proposed reform.

Many debaters think that a counterplan is simply another solution to the problem set out in the motion. It isn't. A counterplan must be competitive with the proposition's plan. The judge should have to choose between the two options. The counterplan must clash with the plan so the opposition can demonstrate that the proposition has failed with its proof. If the plan and counterplan don't clash, the debate ends up as yet another example of the X Y problem discussed in Chapter 5. For example, if the proposition team argued that the federal government should establish new stringent regulations for purchasing handguns and the opposition countered that gun education could reduce gun violence, no clash would necessarily occur. Having tougher handgun regulation does not interfere with having gun education. In fact, these ideas complement each other. The opposition position does not counter the proposition; it is just a different (and irrelevant) idea.

Structuring a Counterplan

A counterplan should include four elements:

- a **detailed description** of the lost opportunity

- an **explanation** of how the opportunity is lost. The argument is also understood to explain how the ideas of the plan and counterplan compete with each other, or clash. This is the reason that arguments about opportunity cost are sometimes called "competitiveness arguments" or "competition arguments").

- a description of the **significance** of the opportunity cost

- a **result**, a comparison of the opportunity cost against any benefits claimed by the proposition team

Let's see how the opposition would develop a counterplan using the universal Medicare example above. The opening opposition speaker would offer *details* of a lost opportunity. In this case, the opposition might say that universal Medicare would inhibit the development of a German-style national health system and describe the primary features of the German model. The speaker would then *explain*, through reasoning and evidence, how the alternative choice is lost because of the proposition plan. In this case, the opposition might argue that a law requiring universal Medicare would make other options illegal. The opposition might also explain that if all doctors, nurses, and other medical personnel, as well as hospitals, labs, and clinics, were included in a universal Medicare system, no health care personnel or facilities would be available for any other health plan. In practical terms, universal Medicare would eliminate the possibility of having any health care alternative.

As with a disadvantage, the opening opposition speaker would next describe the negative *significance* of losing the alternative, noting that the opportunity cost is greater than the proposition team's benefits. In this case, the opposition might argue that not having health care alternatives would limit innovation, potentially leading to higher health care costs, eventually costing U.S. taxpayers millions of dollars.

The presentation of the counterplan, like any meaningful debate argument, concludes with a *result*, an explanation of why the opposition should win the debate. In this case, the proposition's claim that their proposal would do more good than harm and have more benefits than costs is false.

SUGGESTED EXERCISE

Lost Opportunities

For each of the proposals below, name an opportunity that would be lost if the proposal were adopted and explain why that lost opportunity is competitive with the original proposal. You should explain why you can't do both or why doing both would be bad. Here's an example:

Proposal: We should spend Saturday at the mall.

Opportunity Cost: We should spend Saturday at the library.

It's competitive because: If we spend Saturday at the mall, we can't spend Saturday at the library, and we will learn more if we spend Saturday at the library.

- The United States should abolish the death penalty.

- The U.S. should send astronauts to Mars.

- High schools should require physical education for all students.

- Parents should not buy war toys for their children.

CRITIQUES

The opposition can also refute the proposition's solution by offering a critique—an argument that focuses on a major hidden flaw in the proposition's argument rather the effectiveness of the plan. Offering a critique allows you to accept all the facts and evidence that have been presented and concentrate, instead, on the assumptions that underlie them. This kind of careful criticism will produce innovative refutation, new argument lines that reveal that the proposition case may be *more bad than good.*

Once again, let's consider the topic "The United States should make Medicare available to all U.S. citizens." The opposition might claim that the proposition team's case is missing an important element: a connection between the primary causes of illness and access to medical care. The opposition might argue that the causes of illness are environmental pollution, poor sanitation, stress and depression, and bad lifestyle choices. They could argue that access to medical care blinds the public to the reasons why their heath is poor, allowing the underlying causes of illness to steadily worsen. The opposition might try to prove that more medical care would paradoxically produce a sicker society. This argument introduces a different perspective, examining what is missing, in order to show greater costs than benefits.

You can direct critiques at the assumptions associated with an opponent's language, underlying philosophy, and value claims. Think about these particular issues:

- **Language.** Can you make an argument showing that the proposition's language choices might create a bias? For example, is there a difference in describing individuals as illegal aliens and undocumented immigrants? Is there a difference between a freedom fighter and a terrorist? What are the differences and how do they matter? Is a bias enough to undermine the credibility of the proposition's argument?

- **Philosophy.** The proposition might argue in favor of the greatest good for the greatest number—an appeal to utilitarianism. What criticisms are there of utilitarianism? How does utilitarianism protect the rights of minority groups? Are there any uses of the principles of utilitarianism that could do great harm, any historical or contemporary examples of the principle of the greatest good for the greatest number going too far?

- **Values.** These critiques challenge the ethical contradictions or positions that underlie the opponent's arguments. A speaker might advocate peace. But what does she mean by peace? Is it simply the absence of war? Do peaceful societies use peace to prepare for the next war? Could they use nonmilitary means to do great harm to other societies, perhaps through economic sanctions? Are there "peaceful" societies with great injustice—discrimination, hunger, low literacy, public health emergencies?

Structuring a Critique

A critique argument is structured in the same way as a disadvantage. Although there may very occasionally be a specialized exception, in general, critiques should also be unique. They should reveal problems with the proposition's hidden premises that can be used exclusively against their case.

Using Disadvantages, Counterplans, and Critiques

Disadvantages, counterplans, and critiques are usually presented as indirect refutation, although certainly circumstances arise when it is more appropriate or efficient to use them as a form of direct argumentation. A team may introduce one or more arguments in each of these categories in a single debate. In full development, each of these arguments may take some time, and time-speaking limits may reduce the number of these arguments that can be presented in a debate.

Disadvantages, counterplans, and critiques—offensive arguments directed at the solution for one or more social problems—should be a staple of argumentation. Although the opposition side usually uses these tactics, the proposition may also use variations of these arguments to describe the failings of current policy or to indict and refute the opposition.

Refuting the Solution

Create a proposition case for each of the following topics. Identify disadvantages, counterplans, and critiques that might be used against the cases.

Junk food should be banned in schools.

The European countries should bring back capital punishment.

The United States should accede to the International Criminal Court.

Ban bottled water.

Barack Obama should return the Nobel Peace Prize.

NATO should withdraw from Afghanistan.

The United States should require voting.

The United States should adopt English as the official national language.

CHAPTER 12:

EXTENSION AND REBUTTAL

To be successful, a team cannot simply present arguments and refute those of the other side. They must also extend their arguments and offer an effective rebuttal. They must build on their team's critical arguments, and explain to the judge why their team has won the debate.

Argument Extension

Beginning debaters tend to focus entirely on their own ideas and fail to address those of the other side. Intermediate debaters learn to integrate refutation into their speeches while presenting their own ideas. Until debaters have mastered argument extension, they have not reached the advanced level.

Argument extension is the elaboration and development of ideas through several speeches of the debate. It follows refutation. The second and third speakers must engage in argument extension in addition to making and refuting arguments. Do not abandon your partners' arguments unless you are sure that they cannot or should not be revived. Many debates are lost because second and third speakers forget to remind the judge of their teammates' valuable and important ideas.

In extending an argument, debaters use a three-step process:

- **Restate the point.** Briefly summarize the argument in question. No need to repeat the entire point—just mention the highlights so a judge can follow on her flowsheet and take notes in the appropriate area.

- **Amplify the point.** Add something to the argument such as a new example, additional reasoning, significance, or result. Doing so reestablishes the issue as an important one that the other team ignores at their peril.

- **Refute any responses.** This is an opportunity to engage in comparison and evaluation, showing why your argument is more likely to be true than your opponents' answers.

Using the topic "Television is a bad influence," let's look how the proposition might extend an argument. The proposition might argue that television encourages obesity. The opposition team refutes the argument. Argument extension occurs when the second proposition speaker rebuilds the original argument:

- **Restate:** We said that television encourages obesity.

- **Amplify:** This is a major issue because it affects millions of children who will go on to develop serious medical conditions such as diabetes.

- **Refute:** In response, the opposition team said that we should blame parents, not television, but . . .

Debaters should extend the arguments made by their teammates, although they are, of course, free to make their own new arguments (except in rebuttal) and to offer new examples to prove their side of the debate.

In good debates, arguments grow through the process of extension—debaters answer the objections from the other side and use those objections as springboards to flesh out their side's position. Effective debaters choose good arguments initially and make them stronger through the debate rather than simply offering (and likely subsequently abandoning) many different points as the debate goes on.

The Rebuttal Speeches

Rebuttal speeches reiterate the strengths of your case and challenge the validity of the other side's. These speeches are not summaries of the debate. They are a final stand on the floor in which a speaker has the opportunity to effectively assess earlier arguments and reach a favorable conclusion for her team. The speeches are shorter than the constructive speeches—5 minutes for high school PDP debates. New analysis and examples for arguments already established in the debate may be introduced in these speeches but entirely new arguments (those without a foundation in the opening four constructive speeches) are prohibited. Debaters cannot make points of information, although argumentative heckling is allowed.

ISSUE SELECTION

Time is short. Rebuttal speakers must account for all arguments but are unlikely to have enough time to reply to every word spoken thus far in the debate. An effective rebuttalist identifies the key relevant arguments for her side—one or more major issues that might win the debate. The rebuttal speech should make clear to the judge which arguments are IN and which arguments are OUT.

ASSESSMENT

The rebuttal is not a review of arguments, but an opportunity for evaluation, comparison, and assessment of issues to determine if the proposition made their case or if the opposition defeated it. An effective rebuttalist will use all she knows about argumentation and refutation to compare the two sides during her speech and to convince the judge that her side has the stronger position and has, therefore, won the debate. She will also employ all her public speaking skills to ensure an efficient presentation. For example, *word economy*, saying more with less, is a particularly valuable presentation skill for a rebuttal speaker. Because rebuttal speeches must be powerfully expressed, the tactics noted here are particularly valuable at the end of a debate.

The final speaker for the opposition (and for the proposition) should explain ideas using any of the following:

- **Multiple Independent Arguments.** An effective rebuttalist will give her team more than one way to win. It is common for rebuttalists to say to the judge that her team has two or even three ways to win the debate. She will neutralize her opponents' arguments and add an additional issue, Argument Z, to clinch the win. *To be clear, Argument Z may not be a new argument—instead, it can be an existing argument or a comparative claim that establishes superior significance and relevance.*

- **Big Box Theory.** Using this theory, you would explain that one argument is more important than the sum of all arguments from the other side. Easy enough. Winning that one issue wins the debate. A good rebuttalist goes one step further. She explains to the judge at the conclusion of each major argument in her speech why this argument is greater than the sum of her opponents' arguments.

- **"Even-If" Rhetoric.** Even when your opponents have established the legitimacy of their ideas, you can win if you have more to offer. So, a rebuttalist might explain "even if my opponent wins her major arguments, we still win the debate. Here's how . . . "

- **"Reverse Worst Case–Best Case" Rhetoric.** Too many debaters try to summarize the outcome of a debate in the most favorable terms for their side, exaggerating the benefits of their arguments as well as the costs of their opponents' position. A more convincing way to summarize a debate is do the opposite. Make the worst case for your side and the best case for the opponent while still reaching the conclusion that your side wins the debate. For example, the opposition rebuttalist might say "In this debate, let's imagine a completely diminished set of opposition arguments. Let's compare that with the exaggerated claims of the second speaker for the proposition about their case. We are still ahead. Our worst set of arguments is superior to their best case."

- **Comparative Language of the Judge.** Anticipate what the judge might say and say it first. Use that language to evaluate the debate in your team's favor. This will not only convince the judge of your team's superiority, it will also make the judge's task of explaining her decision easier.

ADDITIONAL NOTES FOR REBUTTAL SPEAKERS

Two final notes for rebuttalists

- **Opposition rebuttalists should split the block.** As we saw in Chapter 1, the second opposition constructive and rebuttal speeches function like one long speech, with the two speakers sharing the presentation of the major arguments. An experienced opposition team will divide responsibility equally, with the second opposition speaker and the opposition rebuttal speaker each developing a different argument so well that each speech alone could win the round.

- **Both rebuttalists should avoid the incommensurability problem.** Incommensurability occurs when no basis for common comparison exists or has been offered. Rebuttalists must compare like with like. Who is making the better argument if the opposition rebuttalist argues that a policy will "deprive thousands of people of their right of privacy" and the proposition replies that the policy will also "saves lives"? How could a judge know which team is ahead? Is a clear loss of privacy for thousands of people greater than or lesser than an abstract potential saving of lives?

Rebuttalists must make an effort to transform their idea into a common form to explain issues clearly to a judge. In this case, the opposition rebuttalist could argue that the loss of privacy is so serious that individuals will suffer miserably and actually "envy the dead." The proposition speaker might argue that the ultimate loss of privacy is a threat to one's life. These speakers, once they have established a common basis for discussing the debate's issues, are in a better position to compare the qualitative and quantitative differences of arguments.

ISSUE ANALYSIS FORM

Name: _____

Topic: _____

Date: _____

What do I already know about this issue?

What do I not know about this issue?

Who is affected by this issue? How might they be affected?

Why is this issue important?

SAMPLE TOPICS

High School Public Debate Program Pre-Announced Topics

Political advertising does more good than harm.

California should eliminate Prop 13.

Saudi Arabia is more an enemy than an ally of the United States.

The US should not use economic sanctions in non-economic international disputes.

In selective cases, it is acceptable to punish the innocent to prosecute the guilty.

Governments should not promote gambling.

The US should substantially restrict the immigration of STEM professionals from developing countries.

The international community should establish ad hoc tribunals to prosecute serious labor violations.

The United States should require a national identification card.

Foreign aid does more harm than good.

Indigenous peoples should have exclusive control of their archaeological sites.

Tax religious institutions.

Cyberwar should be prosecuted as a crime against humanity.

NATO should not develop a missile shield.

The world should accept a nuclear Iran.

Governments should not be permitted to assassinate their own citizens.

War memorials do more harm than good.

Political advertising undermines democracy.

Websites should pay consumers for data mining.

The US should substantially increase gas taxes.

California should have drivers' licenses for undocumented residents.

Baseball leagues should ban aluminum bats.

Eliminate personal and religious exemptions for school vaccination policy.

US cyberwarfare does more harm than good.

The United States should block Jihadi websites.

California should legalize internet gambling.

The federal government should not give foreclosure relief to homeowners.

The gray wolf should be a federally protected species.

The United States should implement its European missile shield.

Undocumented immigrants should pay out-of-state tuition at public universities.

California's ballot initiative process does more harm than good.

The United States should have compulsory voting.

Professional sports should legalize performance-enhancing drugs.

Scientists should clone Neanderthals.

The First Amendment should not protect depictions of animal cruelty.

The Obama Administration should release photographs of detainee abuse.

College education should be free.

The United States should abolish the death penalty.

The United States should abolish the Senate.

The First Amendment should not protect depictions of animal cruelty.

The United States should establish a national DNA database for all residents.

Law enforcement should increase profiling based on race and ethnicity.

High School Public Debate Program Impromptu Topics

Schools should not have competitive sports.

The US should arm the Syrian rebels.

Individuals should have a government-issued id to vote.

Ban tipping!

Eliminate the veto power of the UN Security Council.

Zoos do more harm than good.

Schools should not block online access to personal and social media sites.

States should use a lottery of qualified candidates for admission to public universities.

Edward Snowden is more of a traitor than a hero.

The US should prefer Egyptian stability to democracy.

High schools should require a passing grade in calculus for student graduation.

Governments should be obliged to tax the public to pay for war.

This House supports TSA extensive body scans and pat-down searches.

The US should negotiate with terrorists.

The US should elect the president by popular vote.

'Reality television' does more good than harm.

Lower the voting age to 16.

Drone attacks do more harm than good.

On balance, money's influence in politics is beneficial.

The US should substantially reduce trial by jury.

Students should be allowed to carry registered handguns on university campuses.

The United Nations should restrict the right of veto in the Security Council.

It is unethical to eat meat.

The US government should use political assassination to protect national security.

School should be year-round.

US Supreme Court Justices should have term limits.

Schools should punish students for online bullying.

Underage drinkers should receive immunity from prosecution when making 911 calls.

Companies should be able to search employees' personal email and text messages made on company equipment.

The obese should pay more for health care.

Parents should be punished for the wrongdoing of their children.

Individuals should be arrested to failing to help others in an emergency.

Online news is better than print news.

Giving children an allowance does more harm than good.

Peer pressure is more beneficial than harmful.

Schools should be able to discipline students for online bullying.

HOW TO JUDGE DEBATES

Introduction

This manual introduces you to the principles, rules, and procedure for judging Debate Program (PDP) debates. It provides an overview of the PDP format, noting differences between middle school and high school debating, and describes fundamental debate concepts such as argumentation and refutation. The process of judging is discussed in some detail and includes tips for effective decision making and interaction with debaters and audiences. The Public Debate Program website (http://highschooldebate.org/) offers supplemental materials and also frequently updated judging materials.

Every year, thousands of volunteers participate in judging Public Debate Program competitions; not one of their decisions can be characterized as "easy." Fairly evaluating arguments made by enthusiastic and well-prepared students is difficult—even more difficult is explaining the rationale for your decision to the debaters. Assigning individual scores is another challenge. Watching young people participate and work hard to excel is inspiring. Seeing young people become highly conversant on issues of the day is heartening. And, a bit of intimidation (and admiration) can be present when hearing students speak with very few notes on topics that many (or even most) adults would not be able to discuss in an everyday conversation. Nonetheless, judging debates has proven to be rewarding for everyone from college students to retirees and from ordinary citizens to people in demanding careers.

The Principles of Judging

In PDP debates, judging is based on three principles:

- **The judge is unbiased.** Leave your personal ideas and biases at the door. During a debate, the judge does not intervene and speaks only to welcome speakers in order. The judge listens carefully, takes extensive notes, and renders a decision based solely on what the students have said. This can be a revolutionary experience for students and judges alike. Judges learn to listen to young people and practice identifying and removing personal biases. Students are empowered and often transformed by the opportunity to speak from a position of authority to their elders (even if those elders are only a few years older). Long-time PDP coach Anthony Gibson maintains that the very best debaters are often the "back of the class students" or the "disaffected gifted." Students who are silent in class but studious have been known to "find their voice" in debate by simply having the opportunity to speak.

  Often judges will be called on to decide a debate on a topic on which they have strong opinions. It is unfair to students when debates are decided based on what a judge believes rather than on what the debaters actually said. No student can be expected to debate against an adult, especially when the judge's opinions are silent and not subject to refutation or question. When judges intervene in the outcome of a debate by deciding based on their opinions or prior knowledge, they disrespect the efforts of students and contravene the spirit and purpose of educational debate.

- **Students are acting in good faith.** Judges are *not* present in debates to sniff out cheating or other bad behavior. Judges should proceed on the assumption that the debaters are honestly representing the facts to the best of their knowledge. Sometimes judges believe that they are better informed than students or may suspect that students are making up "facts." Without extremely compelling evidence that students are acting in bad faith, judges should respect and honor students' opinions and speeches.

On a number of occasions, judges have come to tournament and program staff complaining about student misinformation only to find out that students knew more about a given topic than their judge. Students conduct topic research prior to a competition (it is self-interested preparation)—judges do not. It may be that more fluid events or more recent reporting have changed the reality (facts). What is also possible is that students used different search terms and research in accumulating facts for a debate. The Internet has such various research matter and sources, with much of it in disagreement. What is also possible is that a fact set known to a judge can be readily countered by a different fact set discovered by a debater. Also, knowledgeable people can simply disagree about what have been presented as facts. For example, many judges thought that debaters made an outlandish claim by arguing that "Iraq does not possess weapons of mass destruction" in debates on the advisability of U.S. military intervention in that country. Turned out that those debaters were right. Debaters identify and challenge opinions and so-called facts.

Because we assume that students are acting in good faith, the Public Debate Program does not have a policy of "disqualification." In many sports, participants can commit fouls or other errors that result in automatically losing the game. This is not the case in the PDP, with one exception: the use of pre-prepared material in debates. Even in this extremely rare instance, judges who notice printed notes on the table before the debate should simply remind debaters (who have likely forgotten or are disorganized) about the rules and let the debate proceed. Students are not ineligible to win if they fail to make points of information (POIs), heckle, or do not use all of their speech time—as you will see below, this only affects their scoring at the end of the debate.

- **Debate is an educational activity.** Tournaments are like learning laboratories. Students learn the principles of debate and material about their topics before the tournament, just as they might learn about chemical reactions in a science class. They practice these skills and try out their ideas at a tournament, just as students go to the lab to see chemical reactions. Sometimes even reasonable adults can become confused about the purpose of tournaments, perhaps because they take the prospect of trophies too seriously. Part of a judge's responsibility is to keep the competitive nature of the event to a healthy background buzz and rise above the fray to make a good decision and educate students about becoming better debaters. As a judge, you are charged with the heavy responsibility of teaching. Try to leave debaters in a better position than you found them, armed with ideas that will help them become more effective and engaged citizens of a democracy.

The Public Debate Program Format

In a Public Debate Program debate, two teams compete against each other. Every debate has a different topic, which is sometimes called the "motion" for debate. It is a short declarative sentence such as "Television is a bad influence." In high school, students receive some topics 3–4 weeks in advance of a tournament but others (called "impromptu topics") are not announced until 30 minutes before a competitive debate.

Before the topic is announced, pairings are posted in a public area used by the tournament for administration and collective announcements. The pairings tell teams which side they will represent in the upcoming debate, which room they will debate in, and who their judge will be. An abbreviated version of a pairing sheet might look like this:

Claremont McKenna Invitational
Round 3—Topic Announcement at 1:30 PM

Room	Proposition	Opposition	Judge
1	Desert Hot Springs ABC	Upland DEF	B. Walters
2	Webb GHI	Oak Hills JKL	K. Couric
3	Compton MNO	Polytechnic PQR	T. Brokaw
4	Sage Hill STU	Rim of the World VWX	P. Jennings

Once you find your name on a pairing, collect your ballot from a tournament administrator. Sample ballots are shown below. The ballot is your primary means of evaluating the debate you are assigned to judge, and you will turn it in to the tournament administrator after the debate.

As the pairings are posted, tournament officials will distribute colored paper to students. An official will announce the topic for debate. Once the topic is announced, debaters will have 20 minutes to prepare their arguments for a preannounced topic and 30 minutes to prepare for an impromptu debate. This period is known as "preparation time," or prep time. During the preparation time, students organize, select, and copy from their notes onto the colored paper and receive coaching advice from their teachers.

In every debate, one team is called the "proposition" team. They argue *for* the motion. They do this by making a case for the motion. The proposition team does not have to defend the motion as being true in all cases. They just have to provide a case for the motion and defend that case successfully against opposition attacks.

The other team is called the "opposition" team—they oppose the case made by the proposition team. To win the debate, the opposition needs to disprove the case made for the motion. They do this by directly refuting the other side's arguments as well as by bringing up new, substantive ideas of their own.

Each team has three debaters. Each debater gives one speech, so there are six speeches in each debate. The first four speeches in a debate are the constructive speeches. In these speeches, debaters work to construct their arguments while refuting the arguments of the other side. The last two speeches are the rebuttal speeches. These speeches give each side a last chance to show why their side should win the debate. Rebuttal speeches should continue the process of refutation. The best rebuttal speakers address all the arguments that have been made in the debate so far and show why the balance of the arguments give the win to their side.

The order of the speeches is as follows:

First Proposition Constructive	6 minutes
First Opposition Constructive	6 minutes
Second Proposition Constructive	6 minutes
Second Opposition Constructive	6 minutes
Opposition Rebuttal	5 minutes
Proposition Rebuttal	5 minutes

There are no breaks between speeches. One of your responsibilities as a judge is to welcome each speaker and to thank each when they are done. For example, "I recognize the first speaker for the proposition,"

"Thank you for the opening speech of the debate. I recognize the first speaker for the opposition."

You are also responsible for timing the debate. So, you should bring a stopwatch or other timer to keep track of elapsed time and give students hand signals indicating time remaining. Tell the students before the debate how you will signal time so they do not become confused during the debate. You are allowed to designate a timekeeper from any of the observers of a debate as long as you are sure that person understands the assigned speaking times. Students are allowed to time themselves if they wish—teammates may time a speaker and a speaker may time herself, but this does not remove your responsibility for timing the debate. An external timekeeper is necessary to ensure that POIs are properly signaled.

POINTS OF INFORMATION

PDP debating uses points of information. A point of information is a request to the speaker who holds the floor to yield some of her time for a point by the opposing team. Debaters may only apply for a POI during speeches made by the other team. Debaters must request points of information and should do so by standing. Debaters may also rise and extend a hand or rise and say "Information." All other verbal applications for POIs—for example, "Point of Information," "Clarification," "On that Point," or "Information, please"—are not permitted. The speaker has a right to deliver a speech without general disruption or continuous verbal applications for POIs.

The speaker may then choose to accept or reject the application for a point of information. If she does not want to take the point, she should gently wave her hand in a downward motion to indicate that the other debater should sit. She may also say "No, thank you." The person applying for a point of information must then sit back down as she does not have the floor. If the speaker chooses to take the point, she may say, "Yes, I'll take your point," or "Your point?" or just "Yes?" If more than one opponent has requested a POI, the speaker should point to the person permitted to make the point or note that speaker by saying "Yes, I will take the first speaker's point."

While more than one person may stand for points at the same time, when a speaker waves her hand or says "No, thank you" that indicates that *all* debaters must sit. If a speaker rejects POIs, she is indicating "I am not accepting points at this time in my speech." Opponents should wait a reasonable time, at least 15–30 seconds or until the speaker has concluded the argument during which she refused POIs, before attempting another POI. Immediately rising after a speaker or his teammate has been refused a POI is inappropriate.

Once the speaker has accepted a point of information, the person making the point has 15 seconds to make an argument, offer a comment, or ask a question of the speaker. POIs do not have to be in the form of a question. Once the person making the point has made it, she must immediately sit down as she no longer has the floor. An opposing speaker does not remain standing during a speaker's reply to a POI. The speaking time of the debater with the floor *continues* during the point of information.

No limits are placed on the number of points any side may try to make during a debate nor are there rules about a minimum or maximum number of points a speaker must accept during her presentation.

You must remember two rules about points of information when you are judging:

- **Points of information are only permitted in the constructive (first four) speeches.**

- **Points of information are only permitted in the middle four minutes of each constructive speech.** The first and last minute of each speech are protected time, and debaters may not make points of information during this time. As the judge, you must signal the end and beginning of protected time by slapping the table once.

- The best way to signal the end of protected time (when the first minute has elapsed) is to slap the table once so that debaters know that they can now attempt points of information. Similarly, you should slap the table once when the last minute of the constructive has begun so that debaters know that any POIs will be out of order. The easiest way to give time signals is with your hands: hold up 2 fingers when the speaker has 2 minutes remaining, etc. When time is up, hold up a fist to indicate that the debater should stop talking.

The above are the only rules the PDP debating has about points of information. A few notes might be helpful though.

- If a speaker loses control of the floor by accepting too many points of information and her speech is therefore disrupted, the speaker is at fault—not the team seeking a strategic advantage. (The Public Debate Program uses points of information to teach students how to manage a dynamic conversation environment.)

- Debaters should take and effectively respond to points of information to help raise their individual score. (This is noted on the scoring rubric.)

- Points of information may be either statements or questions.

- No follow-ups or back-and-forth comments are allowed. Once the debater making the point is finished, she should sit down. If she persists in talking (a very rare occurrence, usually by enthusiastic debaters new to the format), gently tell them that they are out of order.

HECKLING

The Public Debate Program encourages effective heckling during debates. A heckle is an interruption of a speaker during her presentation. Students heckle to applaud teammates and opponents before and after their speeches. This is done by pounding on a desk or tabletop with an open palm or slapping a hand on the table a few times. This is just like regular applause, except the debaters use a desk or table as the "second hand." Supportive heckling is a sign of respect for friends and opponents and shows support for those willing to participate in a difficult competition.

Debaters may also cheer the good arguments of their teammates and show their displeasure with some of the opinions of their opponents. This is known as argumentative heckling. During a partner's speech, slapping the table in support of a particularly clever or winning argument is appropriate. The members of the team supporting the speaker may also add a shout of "Hear! Hear!" to the pounding. During an opponent's speech, it is appropriate to say, "Shame!" if a student strongly disagrees with the opinion of the speaker. Advanced uses of heckling are also permitted, including phrases of up three words offered at relevant points in an opponent's speech. Disruptive heckling—jeering, booing, hissing, or shouting negative comments to the speaker—is not permitted in PDP debates.

Debaters use points of information and heckling strategically to communicate with the judge. They show the judge that an opponent cannot defend an argument or has made an error during a speech. Debaters must use these techniques carefully, however, and should never use them to distract a speaker or continually interrupt a presentation. A judge should score students appropriately for rude behavior during an opposing team's speeches. A judge may also recognize individual speakers and teams for the effective use of points of information and heckling (it is included in the scoring rubric).

Fundamental Debate Concepts

ARGUMENTATION

The argument is the fundamental building block of a debate. Arguments differ from simple opinions. In the Public Debate Program, students learn that every argument has three parts: an assertion, reasoning, and evidence.

The assertion is an argument's topic sentence or main point. "Television shows are too violent" is an example of an assertion. By itself, it is not a complete argument. To support an assertion, students should offer reasoning. Reasoning is the "because" part of an argument. A student might continue his line of reasoning by saying "because television dramas often focus on murder, rape, and assaults." Evidence supports the reasoning of an argument. While there are many kinds of evidence, the most common is an example. A student might support her reasoning by saying "For example, shows like *CSI* or *Law and Order* make it seem like the world is a very violent place and show graphic details."

In addition to making arguments to support their ideas, debaters should explain the importance of their arguments. They do this in two ways. First, they show the significance of their idea. Significance is the quantitative and/or qualitative consequences of their idea. For example, a student might say "This is important, because it can make millions of viewers feel like violence is normal—making them more afraid, and perhaps making them feel like it is acceptable to commit violence themselves." When students explain the result of an argument, they show how it is related to the outcome of the debate: "Because the consequences of violence are so severe, this is more important than the other side's point about the educational values of television." Results establish the relevance of a point in the context of the larger debate, while significance shows the magnitude of a particular argument. The result has been called the "impact" of an argument. But too many coaches, judges, and debaters confuse impact with significance, so result is the preferred term.

Argument Position

Students learn that an argument position consists of these five key steps, summarized as

A-R-E-S-R

Assertion-Reasoning-Evidence-Significance-Result

When judging, remember that not all debaters will offer all these parts for every argument. Students will be more likely both to win the debate and receive higher individual scores if they do, but remembering to make complete arguments in the middle of a debate is extraordinarily challenging. Over time, students do develop the ability to finish their thoughts and show their relevance. Thus, judges must be careful not to "fill in" for students—if a student fails to provide an example, do not provide it for him in your head. Incomplete arguments are not necessarily *false* in a debate. If one side fails to provide reasoning and evidence, the other side has the burden of pointing that out and offering their own rejoinder. Incomplete arguments still stand until they are knocked down; they are just far weaker than their sturdier counterparts appropriately supported by reasoning, evidence, significance, and impacts.

Remember that *just because you think an argument is weak, you may not disregard it.* The opposing team has the responsibility of pointing out weak arguments. Judges should not act as a silent partner, the invisible fourth member of a debate team. Judges listen to the arguments that debaters make and evaluate student performances. One of the major principles of debating is that if an argument is not refuted, it stands. If judges intervene by picking and choosing among what, in their opinion, are the "better" arguments, they deprive participants of the opportunity and responsibility to improve their own practice.

REFUTATION AND THE IMPORTANCE OF CLASH

Good debates are those that have an abundance of clash between arguments and sides. It is not enough for debaters to simply deliver impassioned speeches about their side of a motion. Debaters must also directly and indirectly refute the arguments made by the other side and show why an argument on their side is more compelling than the sum total of arguments of the other side or demonstrate that the balance of arguments gives them the win.

To this end, we teach debaters to use a simple process for four-step refutation:

1. They say . . . " (briefly repeats the argument of the other side)

2. "But they are wrong . . . " (answers the argument of the other side)

3. "Because . . . " (gives a reason for disagreement or counterargument)

4. "Therefore . . . " (explains the consequence of winning this argument)

ARGUMENT EXTENSION

The twin of refutation is **argument extension**, which is the development of an initial idea by subsequent speakers on the same side. To extend an argument, debaters use a three-step process:

1. **Restate the point.** Briefly summarize the argument in question.

2. **Amplify the point.** Add something to the argument such as a new example, additional reasoning, significance, or impacts.

3. **Refute any responses.** Show why the argument is more likely to be true than the opponents' answers.

In good debates, arguments grow through the process of extension—debaters answer the objections from the other side and use those objections as springboards to flesh out their side's position. Effective debaters choose good arguments initially and make them stronger through the debate, rather than simply offering (and likely subsequently abandoning) many different points as the debate goes on.

USE OF EVIDENCE IN DEBATES

In PDP debates, students are encouraged to use evidence—critical to making a good argument. One of the skills we are trying to teach debaters is the use of facts, examples, and other evidence to prove their points. This important skill helps students to conduct responsible research and make informed arguments with good reasoning and grounding in facts and experience.

Debaters may conduct considerable research on topics and topic areas before a tournament. They may also receive a great deal of coaching prior to a debate. However, no published materials may be used during debates; any published information (dictionaries, magazines, etc.) that may have been consulted before the debate cannot be brought into the debating chamber. Debaters may use only those notes made on the colored paper distributed by tournament officials.

Sometimes debaters will include quotations from their research or supporting information from books, magazines, and websites as evidence. At other times, they will support their ideas with examples drawn from personal experience, historical or contemporary examples, or generalizable statistical information. No form of evidence is necessarily better than any other—which evidence is more reliable or more likely to be true is a matter for students to debate, rather than for you to independently evaluate. One common mistake that new judges (and new debaters) make is to assume that because a debater does not cite a source, her evidence is less credible. On the other hand, many people tend to give additional credence to facts where sources are cited. While there can be value in citing a source, it does not *on its own* mean that the material cited is more likely to be true.

Much depends on the nature of the source and how the given facts stack up against others in the debate. For example, if one student says that he learned from CNN's website that no harm comes from currency infla-tion, another student might counter that such has not proved true in many countries, including Zimbabwe and Tanzania. In this case, the latter example may be more credible—it certainly has more in the way of support, especially if the student can explain what happened in those nations. In addition, CNN transmits information but is not, by itself, a source. CNN uses other persons and materials—policy experts, govern-ment officials, reporters in the field, eyewitnesses, business documents, economic forecasts, scientific papers, articles published in academic journals, and more—as sources for its website and broadcast news. Stu-dents citing CNN must refer to the primary source of information, not simply to CNN.

The student citing CNN might respond by saying that CNN is more likely to be correct as it is specifically discussing the United States. At this point, recall the function that evidence serves in debates. It does not necessarily establish a point by itself, rather, it exists as a support for the reasoning of an argument. Here, the students would be well-served to continue comparing their evidence while using reasoning to show why their idea is more likely to be true than false. Just saying or citing "CNN" or "The New York Times" does not make an idea true—this is a common logical fallacy, the *appeal to authority*.

NEW ARGUMENTS

Rebuttals are not the place to make new arguments. This is both a rule and a strategic concern. Entirely new arguments made in the last prop-osition speech are unfair to the opposition team because they do not have an opportunity to answer these arguments.

Now we need to ask: What is a new argument? If an argument has a foundation in the constructive speeches, it is not a new argument. If this is the rebuttal speaker's first opportunity to answer an argument, her response is not a new argument. A new argument is an entirely new line of reasoning introduced in the rebuttal speeches that has no foundation in the constructive speeches.

If an argument is introduced in one of the opening speeches of the debate and that argument is abandoned until the rebuttal speeches, when it is brought up again—that is also considered a new argument. What should you do, as a judge, when you hear new arguments in the rebuttal speeches? Take note of the newness of the argument as it is delivered. Then, when you are mulling over your decision, make sure not let any new arguments factor into that decision.

How to Judge

INTRODUCTION

One element that distinguishes competitive debate from simple disagreement is that in debates two parties attempt to persuade a third, the judge, who deciding the winner of the contest (there are no ties). She also assigns a range of points to individual debaters.

Under the rules of the PDP format, after the debate, the judge tells the debaters how she voted and the reasons for her decision. The judge tells each debater his individual score, explains to each debater a strength to build on and a weakness to work on. The judge will also explain her decision on the paper ballot. These ballots are distributed to the participating teams and their coaches at the conclusion of the tournament.

When you judge a debate, you must choose a winner. Remember: the team that wins the debate may not always be the better debate team; what they were was the better debate team *in the debate that you judged*. Even the best world-class debate teams have critical slip-ups every now and again. You should try to be fair and judge each debate based on its own merits, rather than on speculation, past performances, or other factors including your own opinions about the topic or the arguments students make.

When you begin judging, you may feel unprepared or under-experienced, especially compared with the debaters, who may seem very professional and experienced. However, the debaters have the responsibility of persuading you, the judge. In reality, you are (no matter what your experience level) perfectly prepared to judge a debate. Even if you have never seen a debate before, you can still render a thoughtful and informed decision based only on your engaged participation. PDP debates are meant to be entertaining and accessible to judges and audiences of all experience levels, so even if you are a novice judge, you will fit right in. You will also learn to be a better judge as you watch and judge more debates. Make the best decision you can make and move on.

Although your decision is, by definition, correct, some decisions are nonetheless better than others. Debaters have a tendency to be opinionated. Judges also hold opinions. Holding opinions is normal, healthy, and helps build lively communities. There is, however, a difference between having opinions and forcing them on others at the expense of reasoned debate and discussion. When you judge, make an effort to maintain an open mind about the arguments and examples used as evidence in the debate. Open-mindedness is not so much an issue of surrendering convictions as it is of being respectful of the debaters' opinions and efforts. Remember: PDP debating is switch-side debating. Students do not get to choose their side in the debate. Accordingly, on occasion, you may have the opportunity to watch debaters defend a side contrary to what they (or you) might agree with.

What do we mean when we say that some decisions are better than others? A good decision is one that relies on a consistent, fair method of deliberation and determination. To judge fairly, you need to keep a few things in mind:

- **Remember the three principles of judging.** These are the foundation of your judging.

- **Apply reciprocal standards** for evaluating arguments. Don't hold an error against one team and ignore it when the other team makes it. Make your judging standards relevant and apply them fairly to all debate participants.

- **Be patient.** The debaters may, during the course of a debate, do much that annoys you. They are almost certainly not doing so on purpose. Why would they? You are the one deciding who wins.

- **Give debaters the benefit of the doubt** about their choices—they may not make the choices or the arguments that you would make, but that is okay. Debates are an opportunity to create a place where bright critical thinkers can imagine, analyze, and innovate. If you do not give them the benefit of the doubt, you could end up stifling their creativity or substituting your sense of creativity for theirs.

- **Do not pre-interpret the topic.** It is the debaters task to interpret that topic, and it is *their* interpretation that gets debated. Do not impose your opinion.. If they do not choose to interpret the topic as you would have and argue the case as you would have—that is fine. Your opinions and interpretation should have no bearing on the outcome of the debate.

- **Take extensive notes on your flowsheet.** The debate is decided based on what debaters have said. If you do not write down what they say, you will not be able to make a fair decision. Do not write down your interpretation of what they said, or the gist of what they said, or what they probably meant by what they said. Write down what they said. As much of it as possible. Good judges take extremely thorough notes.

Remember: debaters are *learning their craft*. They may be new to argumentation and public speaking, new to the PDP, new to tournament debating. They might be speaking in a second or third language. Even experienced debaters are still learning to use primary and advanced argument strategies and tactics. And, debate becomes more challenging with impromptu debating for which high school students have no advance notice of the debate topics, thus cannot prepare or research them. Very possibly a debate that does not appear entirely polished may be quite sophisticated because of the way that the students responded to a particularly challenging motion. Judges should not expect perfection, but they should consistently reward serious student effort.

Good decisions are reached fairly with appropriate and adequate deliberation on the issues and arguments that have been presented in the debate.

How should you conduct yourself in a debate? We have already told debaters that they should not treat the judge as if she were merely a passive info-receptacle propped up at the back of the room with a pen and a ballot. Just as the debaters should conduct themselves appropriately toward the judge, so, too, should you act appropriately toward the debaters. The key for the behavior of all participants is *professionalism*—respect and courtesy toward all participants, a commitment to personal integrity and honesty, as well as fairness and tolerance for all, and dedication to an educational mission that includes sharing expertise to contribute to the skills or knowledge of students. The following is a list of "Don'ts" for aspiring and experienced debate judges:

- **Do not discuss how the debate is going during the debate**. Your role should be primarily nonverbal until the debate is finished.

- **Do not penalize debaters who speak in accents other than your own**. Take into consideration that, for some debaters, English may not be their native tongue.

- **Do not introduce personal whim into your role as judge** (e.g., "You must use the words 'x, y, z' in the course of your speeches."; or "Tell a joke and I will give you extra points."). The course and content of the debate are not yours to dictate.

- **Do not arbitrarily manufacture rules** (e.g., "Points of information must be in the form of a question."; "New examples are prohibited in the rebuttal speeches.").

- **Do not write on the ballot during the debate**. This practice conveys a disregard for the competitors and for the integrity of the process. It also makes students feel as if you have already made a decision. Wait until after the debate has ended to make your decision and wait until after the debate to write the ballot.

- **Do not ignore the rules to suit your own preferences.**

- **Do not use marginalizing and discriminatory language or practice** (e.g., comments on ethnicity; sexual innuendo; voting against participants because of their clothes, hairstyle, body piercings, etc.). This rule should go without saying.

The list above may seem long, but you can summarize it in one sentence: Be respectful of the debaters and be fair in your conduct and evaluation of the debate.

Although all judges should follow the rules and try to be fair, there are as many ways of judging debates as there are ways of debating. Judging is an art, not a science. Judges should work to cultivate their own styles and methods of evaluating debates. They should work with debaters to create a learning community that will benefit everyone.

DECIDING WHO WINS

Of course, the critical question is this: How *do* you decide who has won the debate? The best answer is that you base your decision on the criteria the debaters offered. Every debate is about different issues, is conducted differently, and thus should be decided on its own merits. Different teams will offer different kinds of arguments. You must decide: whether the proposition team has made a case for endorsing the motion for debate. The opposition team will offer arguments about why the proposition team's case is inadequate or dangerous or otherwise misguided. You will have to evaluate the merits of these arguments and decide whether the proposition team's rejoinders are satisfactory.

During the course of the debate, debaters may offer suggestions of various criteria for you to use when making your decision. They may even address you directly, saying that your vote should or should not be based on a particular argument set or on certain kind of arguments. This is common practice—do not think that they are trying to order you around. They are trying to both assist you and influence you in your decision-making process.

Do not decide the debate based simply on the number of arguments won by each side. You will also need to evaluate the significance of each argument Take this common scenario: The proposition wins an advantage conclusively, while the opposition wins a disadvantage conclusively. The advantage claims that the proposition's position in the debate would protect Internet and telephone privacy for tens of millions of Americans. The disadvantage claims that privacy protection increases the probability of a successful terrorist attack, although the consequence of the attack is unknown. Who wins that debate? Is it better to protect Internet and phone privacy (although unclear what amount of privacy is lost and what that loss of privacy might mean to an individual) or better to sacrifice privacy for safety (although unclear what the increased likelihood of a terrorist attack might be or its consequences). You would be challenged to decide based on the information we have given you. To answer this question, you need to know the relative significance of the advantage and disadvantage. This relative significance can have both quantitative and qualitative aspects. You may be tempted to decide based simply on the "biggest result." For example, you may decide to vote for the proposition team because they claimed that privacy violations can lead to wrongful arrest, suppression of political dissent, and other consequences that affect the lives of tens of thousands of individuals, while the opposition team was "only" able to prove that that there might be a future terrorist attack but could not establish its likelihood or result.

You also need to take into account questions of risk and probability when deciding who wins in complicated debates. In the above example, your decision would doubtless change if you decided, based on arguments advanced and won by the opposition team, that the probability was low that the proposition team's plan would be able to secure privacy protection. However, this does not mean that you should interject your own risk calculation into the debate. The debaters may have *evaluated* the round for you—they may have made the best case about why their arguments outweigh or are more important than or more instrumental to the decision than those of the other team. If the debaters do compare arguments with one another, you need to take that into account.

One common mistake that judges make is voting for the opposition team on the basis of "partial solvency" arguments. A partial solvency argument is an argument advanced by the opposition team that says the proposition team's case will not solve the problem completely or that the harm or existing problem is not quite as bad as the proposition team claims it is. These are good defensive arguments for the opposition team, but they should almost never be reasons to vote for the opposition team. These arguments prove only that the proposition case is not as good as it was claimed to be. Big deal. It is rare, indeed, that arguments advanced in debates turn out to be just as triumphant as their authors predicted they would be. The proposition team can still win if their case can be shown to be comparatively advantageous—that is, if they can show that it is, on balance, better by some increment than the present state of affairs.

Some judges make the mistake of deciding the debate more or less solely on the quality of the final rebuttal speech. Remember: The proposition rebuttal needs to be evaluated both as a response to the opposition block's arguments and as a summation of the proposition team's final position. When deciding the debate, you need to figure out if the proposition rebuttalist failed to answer any opposition arguments. You then need to decide how to weigh those conceded arguments in the context of the other arguments in the debate.

Often you will have to consider ignored or conceded arguments, also known as "dropped" arguments, and decide what to do about them. If an argument is conceded, then it is assumed to be true for the purposes of the debate. Just because a team concedes some arguments should not lead inexorably to their losing the debate. All arguments are not created equal. Some arguments can be safely ignored.

Other arguments may be introduced in the debate, only to have the team that introduced them later back down on the original claim. This is smart debating and is not a reason to look askance at a team. Debates are dynamic, with students using arguments to test their opponents. Arguments are introduced, adapted, sacrificed, and reinvigorated during a contest. Just as a clever chess player manipulates an opponent through the strategic loss of an important piece, debaters use arguments that might "lose a battle to win the war." For example, it is common practice for opposition teams to offer a wider variety of arguments in their first speech than in their subsequent speeches. On listening to and considering the proposition replies to those arguments, the second opposition speaker then makes choices among her partners' arguments—advancing only those positions that are likely to win the debate and abandoning other ideas that might not help the opposition team or would require a disproportionate amount of time to use successfully. This tactic is called "argument selection" and reveals critical thinking—it is outstanding debate practice. Do not penalize teams for failing to continue every line of argument through the entire debate. Listen carefully to the argument selections of debaters. Students often show that they are discerning and disciplined in the choices made during a debate.

Debate outcomes are decided based solely on the *substance* of arguments. Some students will be more or less effective orators than others. This skill is scored separately in individual points, covered in the next section. We score these separately because even a very poor speaker may be able to win a debate. Consider that debate is like a trial. In a trial, the prosecution makes a case to prove the charge against the defendant. Even the most eloquent lawyer could fail against a stumbling, generally unprepared defense attorney if the defense lawyer was able to prove that her client was out of the country during the time of the crime. Less-experienced debaters or ineffective public speakers might be brilliant analysts. Although the students might be in their first year of high school, they could have superior insight into much older opponents. Those students may be younger debaters but are not younger thinkers. A decision based on the substance of the debate gives them an opportunity to win debates by successfully analyzing the topic—even if they are not as "slick" as their opponents. One side may win a debate even if they get lower individual scores than the other side.

SPEAKER POINTS

In addition to deciding the winners of the debate, you will have to fill out your ballot and assign points to individual debaters. *Speaker points* are a measure of performance by individual debaters. Competitions give awards for team performance as well as speaker awards, which are trophies given to individuals based on their aggregate point accumulation during the course of a tournament. Points are assigned on a 100-point scale using the official Public Debate Program rubric.

You may choose to assign a *low-point win*. A low-point win is a circumstance where the team that won did not get the highest individual speaker points. This circumstance arises occasionally when judges feel that one team did the better job of presentation, but did not win the substantive matter of the debate. *Remember: The total number of points does not decide who won the debate.*

PUBLIC DEBATE PROGRAM

Score	Description	Argumentation
This rubric supplements format and judge certification training and other judging guides.		
59 and lower	59 should be reserved for students who are unsuccessful as debaters as well as otherwise uncooperative, mean-spirited, or disruptive during a debate. This is a most unusual circumstance. Lower points often exclude debaters from awards. If a judge gives a student a score lower than 60, she/he is indicating that the debater, based on this one performance, should be ineligible for any individual or team tournament award.	
60–64	Clearly below average for an experienced debater. This score may be slightly below average for a new or anxious speaker. Lower markings simply indicate that a student has yet to master any of the core elements of debate. A lower score does not indicate a "failure" on the student's part. It is simply an evaluation of the debate.	Does not use the A-R-E (assertion–reasoning–evidence) format for arguments. Offers assertions with little reasoning. Offers little or no evidence to support arguments. Speaker has likely copied arguments from other sources (notes, teammates) but does not understand the issues. Does not amplify partners' arguments.
65–69	This is a below-average performance for an experienced debater but may be a more common "average" score for beginning debaters. Speaker is modestly successful in one major performance element (public speaking, organization, argumentation, refutation, interaction such as POIs and heckling) but is ineffective in other major elements.	Does not generally use the A-R-E format, although there may be an exception for a few arguments. Uses little evidence such as contemporary and historical examples, statistical information or expert testimony. Has inconsistencies, logic gaps, or one or more fallacies in major arguments. Little integration of issues from teammates.
70–74	This is a near-average performance for an experienced debater and a slightly above-average performance for a new debater. Speaker is inconsistent—some speech elements are done well and others are unsuccessful. Speaker may be somewhat unclear about her role, succeeding but leaving opportunities for the other side to exploit.	Speaker clearly understands argumentation but only occasionally uses A-R-E. Speaker is also likely to confuse reasoning and evidence, offering only one of the elements rather than both. Speaker does not make effective argumentative POIs or heckles. Significance established for only 1–2 issues. May struggle to identify the debate's major issues.
75–79	An average to above-average performance. Speaker is competent and does some things well but is just as likely to make errors. This is a good speech—speaker is capable and confident, although style and substance may be inconsistent. Speaker knows her role and tries to accomplish it.	Speaker follows the A-R-E form consistently, although some assertions lack sufficient reasoning and many lack strong evidence. It is more likely that speaker repeats reasoning as evidence. Competently identifies and compares obvious major issues but does not develop nuance or complexity.
80–84	This is a solid, clearly above-average performance. A consistently good debate speech. Speaker appears to be comfortable, eager to participate, and confidant. Inconsistencies in performance are likely to be minor distractions. Sufficiently strong presentation that an ineffective reply will be a serious risk for opponents.	Makes effective arguments throughout the speech. Using the A-R-E format, speaker consistently applies reasoning and, more often than not, also presents evidence to support issues. Appears prepared to discuss the important issues of the debate. Speaker uses argumentative POIs and heckles, although only once or twice.
85–89	An extraordinarily fine speech from a consistently strong debater. Most listeners would say it was "outstanding." Confident and capable—this speech is an effective model for new debaters learning public speaking and debating. May offer innovative approaches to presentation and argumentation.	Speaker is able to establish clear positions that demand a sophisticated reply. Speaker uses A-R-E with highly effective reasoning and consistent application of different varieties of evidence. Explains and analyzes evidence. Establishes qualitative and quantitative significance for all issues.
90–94	Near brilliant. This is an outstanding debater delivering a highly successful speech in *all* respects. Would be a rousing speech for a general audience and a substantive presentation for an audience of field experts.	Not only is speaker able to make powerful arguments, but does so on the spot. The issues are detailed and complex, with substantial evidence to support sound reasoning. Evidence is detailed and well-analyzed.
95 and higher	A MAGNIFICENT performance. Difficult to identify any error. A 98–100 is *flawless*—a combination of Winston Churchill, Barbara Jordan, and Denzel Washington. Maybe one speech in years will score this highly.	Sophisticated understanding of issues and strategies. Develops arguments with multiple causes and consequences. Clever impromptu argumentation. Uses different types of evidence and introduces and analyzes more evidence as debate develops.

Refutation	Structure	Presentation
Does not reply to the overwhelming majority of major points from the other side. Repeats her own arguments without expanding them or comparing them with the arguments of the opposing side. The result little "clash" in the debate.	Disorganized. Does not have a narrative structure to the speech (introduction–body–conclusion). Arguments are not clearly distinguished from one to another. Does not reply to opposing issues in an orderly way, making the speech difficult to follow. Does not use the allotted speaking time.	Distracted, anxious, and halting in delivery. Makes little eye contact—excessive use of notes inhibits establishing a connection with the judge. Mumbles or has numerous vocal pauses "umm," "you know." Disrupts the effectiveness of partners' speeches (interruptions, excessive passing of notes). Either accepts or rejects *all* POIs.
Does not clash with or reply to the majority of arguments from the opposing side. More likely to repeat previous ideas rather than develop, analyze, or compare them. Speaker does not use advanced refutation techniques, for example, evaluating opportunity costs and opponents' underlying assumptions.	Full speech is not well-organized, although one or more individual points may be appropriately organized. Lacks an attention-getting introduction and a powerful conclusion. Difficult to follow for a significant amount of time. Unclear when moving from one point to another. May use full speaking time, but ineffectively allocate time to key issues.	Loses clarity for sustained periods. Poor eye contact and infrequent use of gestures. Speaker does not sound confident or convincing. Rarely attempts a POI and is distracted by POIs from the opposing team. Does not work effectively with teammates or participate in positive or negative heckling.
Speaker is much more likely to discuss her/his own arguments than answer an opponent's arguments in a direct and forceful way, although there is some refutation of limited effectiveness. Speaker offers more general refutation rather than combination of general and specific counters. May compare some competing issues not consistently.	Speaker has a basic structure (introduction, body, conclusion) but strays from it during presentation. Speaker is likely to be able to organize her/his own arguments but loses structure when trying to address opponent's points. Speaker gets distracted or slows the pace too much when confronted with POIs/heckles. Could allocate time more effectively.	Speaks clearly but there are noticeable pronunciation or other verbal errors that are sufficiently distracting for the audience or disrupt the natural flow of the speech. Speaker makes POIs but they are generally obvious questions, not carefully considered or analyzed arguments. Does not attempt or succeed at effective heckling. Good but not outstanding nonverbal communication.
Understands her own positions but spends too much time repeating those ideas rather than developing them. Unlikely to establish qualitative (matter of degree) and quantitative (number affected) significance. Unlikely to compare with opposing views. Uses direct refutation well but offers little advanced refutation.	Organized and generally effective. Attempts a narrative structure but is not able to consistently adhere to it at one or two points of the speech. Loses some clarity integrating opposing arguments. Uses time effectively—speech is balanced with an appropriate mix of arguments and refutation.	Speaks in a clear, comprehensible way. Effective nonverbal communication (eye contact and gestures). Style is competent but not supremely confident. May speak in a monotone. Attempts 1–2 POIs and gives reasonable but unspectacular answers to POIs. Attempts effective heckling.
Maintains her own or team's positions, supplementing them with thoughtful analysis and examples. Has more difficulty with opposing team's arguments but is able to effectively refute most of their major arguments. Speaker primarily uses only direct refutation (simple disagreement) but is effective.	Simple, effective narrative structure for own arguments but has some difficulty integrating multiple counter-positions into speech. Uses speaking time effectively—uses full amount of time and appropriately allocates time to important issues. The speech is sufficiently organized so that listeners not taking notes could follow it.	Speaks in an engaging manner—clear but only occasionally highly entertaining and powerfully persuasive. Confident and credible. Concise POIs have clear relevance to the debate. Occasional verbal pauses ("umm . . .") do not distract. May be ineffective or confusing at 1 or 2 notable times. Strong eye contact.
Speaker uses direct refutation and advanced refutation techniques, including opportunity cost evaluation, strategic agreement, and turn/capture of opponent's positions. Outstanding expressions of significance and impact assessment with opposing side's major arguments.	Logical organization that is easy to follow and flow. Likely to have effective intro and conclusion. Able to organize own positions and opponents' into a well-integrated speech. Can use all speaking time but may not because of efficiency. May use nonlinear structure without losing clarity.	An animated speaker able to present a clear and convincing case. Persuasive and credible. Excellent integration of public speaking skills, including nonverbal and verbal skills. Strong public speaker in all but one notable respect. Strong POIs and replies to POIs. Infrequently distracted by other team.
Understands how arguments interrelate. The speaker investigates inconsistencies among opponent's claims. Identifies and exploits opportunity costs and underlying and hidden assumptions.	Strong narrative or clever alternative structure. Persuasive introduction and conclusion. Speech is sophisticated, yet easy to follow and understand. Seamlessly integrates arguments from both sides.	Effectively uses rhetorical devices like humor, effective pausing, and vocal inflection to add substantial depth to speech. Thoroughly engaged—speaker attempts many clever POIs. Highly effective heckling.
Integrates advanced refutation into argumentation, using ideas from opponents to advance speaker's own side. Uses POIs and heckling as opportunities for powerful refutation. Accounts for or has an outstanding reply to every important opposing point.	Develops a clear, well-organized (effective narrative or other structure), and efficient speech. Despite argument complexity, nearly any listener could follow the speech. Speaker capable of restoring order to even a confusing debate.	Has exceptional subject knowledge, delivered in a highly entertaining and informative manner. Brilliant verbal and nonverbal skills, including eye contact, volume, pace, clarity, and humor. Speech would make an ideal demonstration.

USING THE SPEAKER POINT RUBRIC

The rubric is based on what we have learned over the years about effective educational assessment. It is periodically updated, so this rubric may not exactly match one you receive at a tournament, but the concepts will remain the same. Always check with the tournament director to ensure that you are using the current version of the rubric. It is a *content-based* rubric, not a *norm-based* tool. Grading based on norms seeks to find an average performance and assign all students relative to that average. Meaningful scoring in debates does not work this way. In theory, all students can aspire to receive a perfect score, as scores are assigned based on what students actually *do* in a given debate rather than on some hypothetical comparison with all of their peers. Topics, sides, and opponents change, thus norm-based scoring is unreliable—and therefore unfair—in debates, although it is the most popular approach to debate scoring across secondary school debate formats.

Although the scoring range is 1–100, notice that scores of 59 and lower are strongly discouraged. Those scores are reserved for students who are both unaccomplished debaters *and* disengaged from the process, unprofessional, and hostile to teammates and opponents. Accordingly, these scores are extremely unusual. If you assign a score below 60, tournament officials will likely ask for an explanation as it indicates a potentially serious problem at the event.

Scores at the top of the rubric are likewise extremely rare because debating is such an extraordinary challenge that giving a 90–100 point performance would be most exceptional. To give a score this high is to assign our program's most prestigious award and happens only every few years. It is exceptionally difficult for high school students to have developed and then employed the skills necessary to achieve this score in an impromptu debate.

The rubric has six columns. The first column indicates the score range discussed in a given row. The next column offers a general description of that score range. The following columns are argumentation, refutation, structure, and presentation. These are given equal weight and you should assign scores accordingly. A student might be in the 70 zone for presentation and argumentation, but in the 60 zone for refutation and structure. That student should receive a score in the middle, around a 65.

You do not have to turn in the rubric after debates—students already have copies of it. The rubric is to help them improve. The Public Debate Program thrives on transparency and accountability. This is why judges are asked to reveal and explain their decisions and grading. Students will consult their copies of the rubric to "find themselves" on the chart. We encourage them to look at the rows above their score to see how they can improve. Debaters should take their scores, a copy of the rubric, their flowsheets, and teammates' notes and recollections of the debate, as well as notes made when the judge explains the decision after the contest, and use these to reengineer a team's performance. Using this material, students should be able to track their skill development across various debates that involved different topics, arguments, opponents, and judges. They can use the rubric to identify strengths and weaknesses. Teachers and coaches can assist students to engage in this kind of self-assessment after each tournament competition. It is the equivalent of reviewing athletic performance by watching videotape of the contest or reading coaching reports.

Assigning students their "true score" is extremely important. Sometimes judges hesitate to give scores on the low range of the scale because they are worried about hurting students' feelings or because they are simply so impressed with students' performance that they want to say "good job!" But it is very common to assign scores on the low end, especially for new debaters.

"Point inflation" has individual and social costs. Assigning higher scores hurts students rather than helping them. It is the equivalent of social promotion. Students get a false sense of their own skills and are unlikely to work as hard to improve. Social costs are also incurred—if students randomly draw judges who assign higher scores, the awards at the end of the tournament will be unfair as they will be biased by the effects of random judge assignment rather than the result of students' hard work.

The rubric can be intimidating because of its sheer volume of words but does need to be carefully reviewed before the tournament. As you judge more debates, you will become more familiar with the scoring ranges and their rationales. **Avoid the temptation to judge based on the second column**. Some new judges will default to the "description" category because it is simply easier and quicker. This is neither an effective nor correct way to assign students' scores. Relying on the description column has judges skating closer to the language of "average," "below average," and "above average"—precisely the kind of norm-based assessment the rubric is designed to correct.

Each student receives his own score. Two or more students may receive the same score in a debate, sometimes for very different reasons. As a reminder, scores do not determine the winner of a debate.

TAKING NOTES IN DEBATES

Flowsheet 1

1st Proposition	1st Opposition	2nd Proposition	2nd Opp/ Opp Rebuttal	Prop. Rebuttal

Flowsheet 2

Townsend Showdo

January 22, 2005

Valerie-on

1st Proposition	1st Opposition	2nd Proposition	2nd Opposition	Proposition Rebuttal
Chelsie 27	Brandon 28	Chaithra 27.5	Kevin 27	Richard 27.5
Boxing - legalized way of attacking another. toe to toe → hit till knocked out. Football etc → other goals - this sport exc. blows to the opp. may say fit, but ↓ later - 2nd ! synd. Car moving - brain is passenger. [Why so popular?] - Brit/Amer. consid. ban. Norw/Swed. alr. ban boxing. - Why ↓ crime? Boxing → influence to fighting. → rest of lives - hypocrisy - Protect Boat Scotland - - Ban → less people hurt + die. - stop = ↓ crime - boxing is barbaric - in the ring it's suddenly OK? - hurts children	→ It's a sport - well respected sport - Hockey, Football, etc - indirect attention - exc. - hit the guy - penalties - 3 foul blows, 3 hard shots → out. - medics in every corner / breaks - ∅ barbaric - it's a sport. - make so much $ that - are fit → good health → role models. [boxing → ∅ use their words] - it's not like wrestling - → try to ban it - Ali, boxes, but his daughter does too - Bacho Camacho. too - → hockey ports → arrested - flip over head → arrested. had no alt - provided for family while boxing -	How many deaths before boxing is banned? [in the ring there are medics] ▸ slavery was a tradition; ∅ OK. ▸ more people hurt in boxing. [BAN = UNDERGROUND] ∅ like murder ▸ boxing - gambling illegal → copying. → no, SI showed → exploited + most injured. → still people lose their lives - 1st 2nd ! syndrome. → profs/legend → Ali lost. Lionel Tate. → banning boxing → ∅ feel pressure to box ↓ pressure on Laila. → $7K ∅ enough to show for it.	→ Lionel Tate → → wrestling - ∅ relev. to boxing. wrestling soap opera → safety / reg. → everything they say is true - w/o gloves, medics, etc. → much more ↑ illegal gambling. [then should we leg. drugs or murder?] ↓ Olympics → clean + safe. [Honor? - Gladiators ∅ honored - ∅ talk about] Norway honor + safety Moh. Ali Act / Boxing Ref. Act. → make safer. Medics may ∅ work but better to have safety [Betting, etc →] → black market ∅ safety, ∅ more trained refs, ∅ more breaks, etc. → OK, those are our args. - safety → as watching ... often. → ban boxing - thous of. B. Scotlands. - ∅ ban it - leave it. hockey + soccer → ... same	- Goal in hockey → ball - football, goal is to have - How many? 1 is enough. → Drugs underground, we ∅ leg. that. Norway + Sweden have less crime - Ban boxing = won't get Parkinsons disease → ↓ crime, better lives - barbaric; like Gladiator. ↓ violence; ↓ crime - IE Norway + Sweden. → ∅ bans 2nd ! syndrome.

Flowsheet 3

First Proposition Constructive	First Opposition Constructive	Second Proposition Constructive	Second Opposition Constructive / Opposition Rebuttal	Proposition Rebuttal
Boxing = legalized attack of a person (knock out)	Boxing is well-respected	1. Stop freedom of children boxing	1. We should ban wrestling instead (all and fate is violent)	1. Boxing has a more dangerous sport than other sports ex. soccer
1. Boxing has a violent goal, unlike other sports (ex. contest), it hits ben courses, ex. football, does not have this	2. Other sports have subcategories violence ex. football, hockey tackle/check	2. Sports III, fund boxers are exploited, most inj...	2. Underground boxing = more deaths/injuries, scabbing [Drugs are still likes.]	2. Scotland/Ali must not be ... again
2. Injury/bad health ex. Parkinsons (2) second-impact syn.	[No punches in boxing?] (yes, there are rules)	3. Scotland's death, other (like this are bad)	3. No safe way to do drugs, there is safe boxing	3. Bludgeround does not mean we shouldn't legalize
[Why does boxing thrive?]	[Don't punch kids with up?]	4. Boxing wouldn't be okay on the street. (heat, thermetical)	[Gladiators were band.] 4. Gladiators were in Roman times (illegal)	4. Less crime in Norway/Sweden due to ban
b. popularity has been down ex. Norway/Sweden banned boxing	b. There are rules and medics	[Isn't about safety in the ring?]	5. Take honor out of boxing, murders	5. Children should not follow boxer's footsteps, boxer's life
3. Illegal in real life ex. arrested for boxing on the street	3. Old boxers retire/ boxers are fit/ promote good health	b. People see it on TV and do it outside of the ring	[It's illegal on the street] negotiators/medics make it's safe	6. Less death/better it
4. Scotland's death, violence injury, stop brainwashing, barbarity	[Shouldn't we teach kids out violence?] b. Kids shouldn't box after a match	7. Traditions aren't always social slaver	[Medics don't help] b. Better some than no help	7. Barbaric > gladiators
5. Boxing has death, *safety of path help	4. Don't know much abt banned sports ex. children of boxers box	[Underground = more death] b. No way we shouldn't ban it, still a decrease	Billion dollar empire [Merged] [Merged]	8. less crime/death in Norway/Sweden
	5. Every sport can have illegal actions on the street ex. football tackle	5. ↓ crime ex. illegal gambling violence	4. Lost jobs, more violence, more death	9. Dropped, 2nd impact syn.
	6. Scotland was a loss	[What about violent video games?] b. Relevant, bears Gatesham	1. Underground death and sports regulation	a. Scotland is dead, not repeal
	a. Police soldiers	[Boxing isn't better/ it's worse] Death	2. No more safety w/ evidence.	
		1. head = only death 2. Injury/brain damage	3. Can't enforce this/ can't crime stop/ other sports have violence	
			5. wrestling is staged 6. Boxing is not covered, regulated	

Taking notes in debates is called "flowing." For debates, all students and judges use a graphic organizer called a "flowsheet," which is divided into columns representing different speeches in a debate. Traditional note-taking strategies are ineffective for debating or for fairly judging a debate because debates are about the relationship between arguments and their give-and-take (thus the word *flow*) during a debate.

Flowsheet 1 shows a blank flowsheet. Notice that there are six speeches in a debate but only five columns, which are labeled by speech. Why? Because there are two opposition speeches in a row; the second opposition constructive speech is immediately followed by the opposition rebuttal speech. These speeches, often called the "opposition block" function as a unit, responding to the points of the second proposition, extending the points of the first opposition, and summarizing the debate. The proposition rebuttalist will respond to these speeches as a unit; thus, judges and debaters take notes for these speeches in the same column. Sometimes you may need more space to take notes—simply flip over your flowsheet and continue in the same column on the other side.

Flowsheets 2 and 3 show completed flowsheets. They are from two experienced judges who watched the same sample debate. Note the differences in style. Each judge has worked to write as much as possible (both flowsheets continue on the reverse side—not reproduced here). Note that Flowsheet 2 has some numbers on the top of each column. These are speaker points that remain from a prior scoring system that the Public Debate Program no longer uses.

The flowsheet is your record of the debate. Nobody will look at it but you, so it is okay to use shorthand that might be hard for others to decipher. In theory, you should be able to use your flowsheet to reconstruct the debate, thus it should be thorough and accurate. Here are a few guidelines for effective flowing:

1. **Write down as much as possible**. Sometimes judges are tempted to write their interpretations of what students said or what students "meant"—don't do it! Remember you are to judge the debate on

what students actually said, not on your interpretations. Sometimes, judges write down only what they think is important. Again, this is a mistake. What you think is important is not necessarily what the students see as important—particularly as the debate goes on. If the rebuttal speeches focus on an earlier argument you considered irrelevant and so did not transcribe, you will be unable to make a fair decision. When in doubt, err on the side of writing everything down.

2. **Use abbreviations where you can**. Every judge and debater develops her own set of abbreviations. Instead of writing out the word *money*, use a dollar sign. Instead of writing out *not*, use a circle with a slash through it. Abbreviations will help you get more information down as students proceed.

3. **Use visual connectors to show interaction of ideas**. In debates, students respond to one another's ideas and extend on their team's lines of argument. It is essential to note those connections on your flowsheet. The best way to do this is by using circles and arrows, as in Flowsheet 2. When a student refers to an argument from an earlier speech, connect it across the flowsheet to the current column using a line or some other indicator.

4. **Put arguments next to the ones they go with**. One of the major differences between the Flowsheets 2 and 3 is that Flowsheet 3 has many very long arrows. The judge did this because students addressed previous arguments in a new order and the judge wanted to note connections. Although noting connections is essential, making very long arrows can be confusing and impair your ability to track the ebb and flow of ideas in a debate. As a rule, hew more closely to the strategy in Flowsheet 3. Here, instead of transcribing the speech as it happens and weaving a complicated network of arrows, the judge has put refutation or extension ideas vertically near the ideas they relate to. This makes it easier to see points of clash. It will also help you see when arguments have been conceded because there will be blank space next to them.

5. **Flow points of information in the column of the speaker who holds the floor, noting responses where appropriate.** Notice that, in both of the completed flowsheets, judges have put items in brackets in some speeches. These indicate that the speaker took a point of information. Points of information are part of the debate and should be part of its written record. When a speaker accepts a point, simply make a bracket and note the statement or question from the other side. Then close the bracket and note the speaker's answer. Some judges track the number of times that a student attempted POIs by making hash marks in the appropriate student's column, while others simply remember or use a different notation system, such as a separate piece of paper to record POI attempts and contents/replies.

Like any skill, flowing takes time to master, but it is easy for most judges to immediately pick up. The key is to write as much as possible so that you can make a fair decision. In addition to helping yourself, you are also being a good role model for students learning the essential skill of note-taking.

After the Debate

Once the debate is over, you should thank both teams for their participation and invite them to step outside the room while you make your decision. This way they can meet each other and let off a little steam and you may decide in peace. Take no more than 5–7 minutes to decide the debate and assign points. Although your ballot asks you to write a rationale for a decision, it is enough to simply write a sentence or two now; you will have time in a few minutes to finish your written decision.

Once you have decided, invite the students back into the room. Use your timer and take no more than five minutes to speak to the students. Begin by giving the debaters any general feedback that might apply to both sides ("Both teams could use more evidence to support their opinions"), announce which side won the debate and why: "In this debate, the XXX team won because of YYY." Use the students' arguments from the debate to explain the outcome. It should be comparative:

> The proposition used two arguments to support the case and the opposition only challenged one of them. Although the challenge was partly effective and the opposition correctly pointed out that the case was diminished, the case was still made. As the final proposition speaker remarked, the second argument was not answered and that argument was every bit as important as the first argument. That alone won the debate. But the proposition was still able to prove a portion of their first argument—even the opposition admitted that. And that also proved the case, although in a small way. The opposition offered no other arguments. So the proposition won on either of their two arguments.

Then, addressing each student by name or position, give the individual score ("The first proposition speaker received a 72, second, 75, third 73. The first opposition speaker had a 71, second, 70, and third, 68."). For each team and student, you should tell them one or two things they did well and one or two things they should work on. Five minutes will pass quickly—be efficient.

Some tournaments have more time for feedback. A tournament official will let judges know how much time they have to deliberate and give feedback before surrendering their ballot to the tournament tabulation desk. You can, of course, invite students to ask more questions and speak with you later in the day, but you will need to bring your ballot to the tournament officials to record the results after the announcements at the end of each debate to keep the tournament on schedule.

One common mistake judges make is using "I language" after the debate. Judges will say "I was convinced that . . . " or "I was persuaded . . . " or "I agree that . . . " but this is not good practice. Sometimes when judges use "I language" often during their explanation, students leave the debate thinking something along the lines of "That judge voted against me because of their opinions" rather than taking your decision and advice to heart. Try to phrase your comments to students in authoritative, declarative sentences. For example, instead of "I found this argument persuasive because . . . " say "This argument was good because . . . " or "The opposition argued that government action would produce a severe unintended consequence that would harm more children than would be protected and the proposition did not challenge that premise or consequence. The proposition only said XXX, which did not clash with the opposition argument."

Sometimes when we talk to students our instinct is to "soften the blow" of a decision by saying that this was "just" the decision that we made. This way of framing your decision is, in truth, an obstacle to helping students learn how to lose debates.

Another common mistake that judges make is offering rationales that are far too general. Judges may say "The proposition won this debate because they had better arguments and proved their case." This is not a good reason for a decision. It could be true of any debate, no matter the topic and specific content. When judging a debate, make sure to mention specific ideas. You might say "The proposition won this debate because they showed that the benefits of homework outweigh its costs. Their strongest argument was . . . " Mentioning specific ideas and showing students how you evaluated them helps debaters improve. It also anchors your decision in the actual language of the debate, helping to prevent you from journeying down the dangerous road of personal preference.

Writing Your Ballot

When you are done with post-debate interactions, you must return your ballot to the tournament administrator. Do not delay the tournament—if you wish to continue talking to the students, tell them you will speak to them after your ballot is completed.

When you return your ballot, the administrator will check it and enter your result and scores. If the ballot section that asks a judge to write feedback about the debate is blank or incomplete, a tournament official will return the ballot so that you can complete your written rationale.

It is important to do a good job of writing a ballot. One of the most important aspects of a debate is the feedback students receive from a judge. Debaters look forward to and value the comments judges make on their ballots. To help students improve and also help them understand the reasons for the judge's decision, a judge needs to provide useful comments, a thorough analysis of the round, and the reasons for the decision.

The ballot is also an outstanding tool to communicate direct feedback to teachers/coaches. Ballots can be particularly helpful where a judge has evaluated several teams from the same school and the students make a common error (e.g., they might believe that POIs are acceptable in the rebuttal speeches). The written ballot can help correct the common problem by communicating that error to the school's coach. If the judge only gave that information verbally to individual teams in each debate, the students might not mention it to the coach and thus the coach would remain in the dark.

Although ballots have no universal formal structure, certain elements are key to a good ballot: the reason for decision; comments directed to specific debaters; and comparisons of arguments made during the round are especially useful to debaters. Make sure to point out what each team could have done better and recognize what they did well. Encouraging debaters to improve and to continue competing is just as important as providing critique. Any communication to a teacher/coach is helpful. Below is a list of do's and don'ts when preparing a ballot.

Ballot Checklist:

- Be thorough
- Provide reason(s) for decision

- Tell debaters what they did well and what they could do to improve

- Discuss and compare arguments made during the round

- Provide a thorough analysis of the debate

- Use constructive criticism

- Provide helpful information for the coach

- Write neatly

What Not to Do:

- Do not "flow" on the ballot

- Do not leave the ballot blank or incomplete

- Do not leave out your reason(s) for decision

- Do not list arguments without commenting on them

- Do not write illegibly or use too many abbreviations

To help you understand how to structure your comments and what type of information to include, we have provided examples of two very good ballots given to students at tournaments.

The first ballot clearly states the reason for decision in the first sentence, going on to give some advice to both teams and each individual speaker. In the second sample ballot, the judge takes a slightly different approach, exploring in depth the arguments of both teams, explaining how they played out against each other in the debate, and finally comparing them as the students have argued. Each style is good and helpful to students. As a judge, you will develop your own style for writing ballots.

Sample Ballot 1

IN MY OPINION, THE TEAM THAT WON THE DEBATE WAS THE
(CIRCLE ONE) (PROP.) OPP.

SIGNATURE: _Rebecca L Peacock_ AFFILIATION: _____CMC_____

PLEASE USE THE SPACE BELOW TO INDICATE YOUR **REASON FOR DECISION** AND TO PROVIDE HELPFUL COMMENTS TO THE DEBATERS.

I voted for the proposition today because they were able to tell me why the status quo had health care problems that the resolution would begin to solve for, while the opposition did not fully explain why the current health care system was good enough and why government funding to other programs was more important.

Both teams need to work on explaining their points more, then they would speak for a longer period of time, and counter the other team's points.

Prop #1: Good volume and clear speaking. You need to explain your points more—why is the current health care system bad?

Opp #1: Good clear speaking and off-case points. You need to counter the proposition's arguments!

Prop #2: Good extensions. However, don't let points of information dominate your speech, and address the opposition's arguments.

Opp #2: Good explanation and extensions of your team's points, but why are they better than universal health insurance and why are the problems that universal health insurance brings worse?

Opp #3: Good summary of points and eye contact. You need to emphasize why what you represent is better.

Prop #3: Good summary and good job beginning to counter the opp's arguments. You also need to tell me why your side is better.

Sample Ballot 2

IN MY OPINION, THE TEAM THAT WON THE DEBATE WAS THE (CIRCLE ONE)   (PROP.)   OPP.

SIGNATURE: _Howard L. Johnson_ AFFILIATION: _____CMC_____

PLEASE USE THE SPACE BELOW TO INDICATE YOUR REASON FOR DECISION AND TO PROVIDE HELPFUL COMMENTS TO THE DEBATERS.

This is a low-point victory:

The prop won 3 uncontested points:

1. 60% of those executed are innocent

2. blacks are executed disproportionately to whites

3. The U.S. should set an example for other nations.

The opp won 2 points, though not strictly:

1. The death penalty will deter crime (though how much life imprisonment will deter lessens this

2. The guilty who are executed get what they deserve (example of Westerfield was used).

*For the record the opp came out on the favorable end of two other issues:

1. the biblical debate on an "eye for an eye"

2. Tax $ issue though it was never really quantified.

The three uncontested points, on balance, outweigh the points won by opp. Nothing the opposition said justifies the deliberate execution of innocent people by the government.

Notes on Audiences

As its name implies, the Public Debate Program is designed to teach students to debate in front of audiences. Because debates are fun to watch, most of the debates you judge at tournaments will have audiences. Sometimes these will be quite small—students from the host school or a few parents. Sometimes you might have several dozen spectators at a debate. Judges and debaters are not permitted to restrict viewing of a debate unless a spectator is disruptive.

Audiences are permitted to use only supportive heckles during debates. They should, at the very least, support the speakers as they take and leave the floor. They are not permitted to cue students. If you suspect that this kind of behavior is happening, gently remind the person in question that it is not allowed. Usually it is an overexcited parent or sibling who does not intend to skew the outcome of a debate.

If an audience member is disruptive, the judge may call a debate to order simply by saying "Order," or "Order, please." This is normally sufficient to stop audience disruption. There are a few occasions when overly excited students speak well above a whisper to teammates and it interferes with a judge's ability to hear a speaker. It is appropriate for a judge to gently call "Order" to make sure that the debaters know that they should speak more quietly. The judge does not call for order to protect a speaker from multiple POI attempts or opponents' heckles. Students manage those elements of the debate on their own.

Although audiences are encouraged to watch debates, they are not permitted to dispute the decision of the judge. In fact, they are not to talk to the judge at all after debates. Sometimes even comments that seem like friendly questions ("I was just wondering how you felt about this particular argument . . .") are thinly veiled pretexts for criticism. We wish it were otherwise, but the fact is that parents and often coaches can sometimes take the competition element of a debate tournament too seriously for their (and their students') own good. If someone tries to engage you about your decision, it is appropriate to gently remind them that you are not allowed to discuss your decision with observers.

Procedures are in place for disputing judges' conduct or decisions. A judge's decision is final, but from time to time parents may wish to provide feedback on judges to the tournament. They should not speak to the tournament director, but should speak to the coach of their affiliated school. The coach will then speak to the tournament director.

On occasion, the tournament director might approach a judge to offer some constructive support to improve judging practice. This is normal and helpful for most judges, who should not take it as anything other than an attempt to help them improve their craft.